Cosmic Duality

Cosmic Duality

By the Editors of Time-Life Books

TIME-LIFE BOOKS, ALEXANDRIA, VIRGINIA

CONTENTS

The Unity of Opposites

In the beginning, God created the heaven and the earth," recounts the biblical Book of Genesis. "And the earth was without form, and void; and darkness was upon the face of the deep. . . . And God said, Let there be light: And there was light. . . . And God divided the light from the darkness. . . . And the evening and the morning were the first day." Creation seems to imply contrast: Light reveals darkness; morning ends the night. As the Genesis story unfolds, other universal opposites emerge: male and female, good and evil, and finally life and death. These and other paired energies dominate creation tales around the world.

For most societies, however, the great dualities of nature are not unalterably opposed. Instead, such forces combine and intertwine. In the sacred artifacts pictured here and on the following pages, light confronts darkness, the genders commingle, and death dances with life in scenes of rebirth and resurrection. Even good and evil are conjoined in such ambiguous figures as the snake—to some cultures a magical symbol of health and good fortune, to others a harbinger of malice and deceit.

Nineteen feet wide and twenty-three feet high, this seventh-century carving honors the Hindu god Shiva, a multifaced deity in whom all opposites combine.

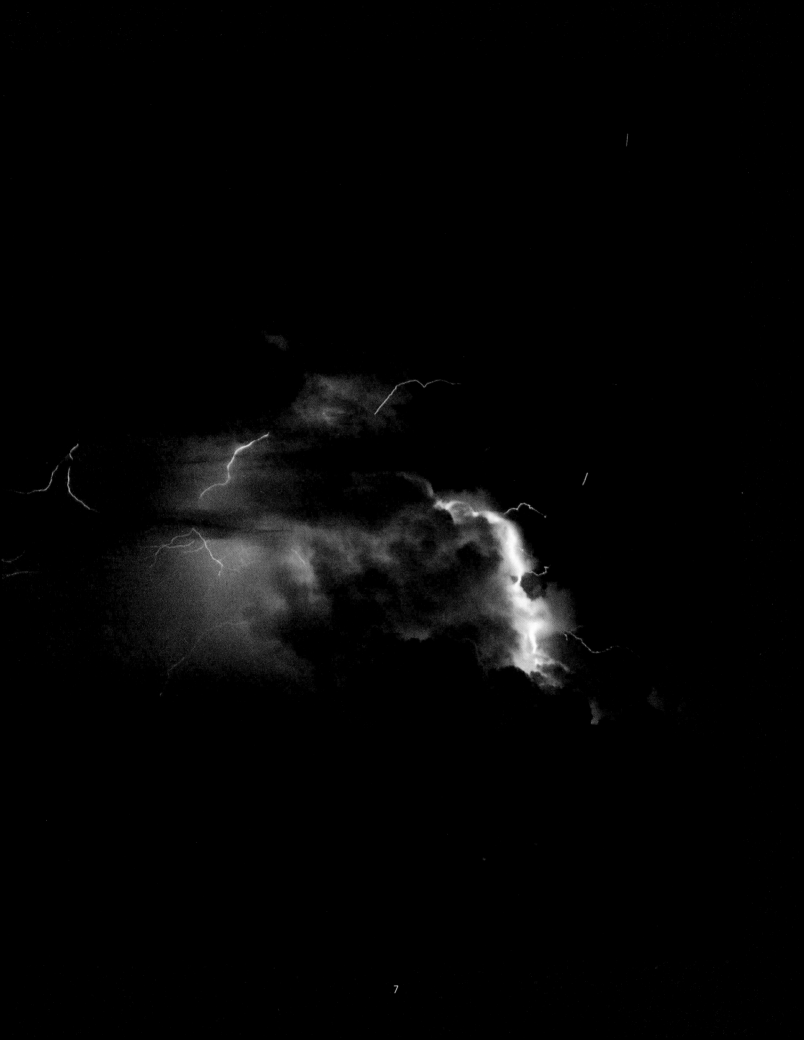

Paired dragons guard the pin-wheel emblem of yin and yang in this eighteenth-century Viet-namese mother-of-pearl inlay (left). Each of the two forces, locked in harmony as much as in opposition, holds the seed of its opposite: The dark yin contains a tiny speck of yang, and the paler yang embodies an embryonic germ of yin.

Half black and half white, Shiva balances atop a tamed demon and a bull—respective tokens of death and fertility—in the seventeenth-century Hindu painting above. Powerful be-cause he unifies all opposites, Shiva is at once the source of maternal gentleness as well as of the warrior's strength.

A symbol of masculinity and the procreative force, this stone linga from eastern India is also said to represent the original cosmic egg, because it has no flat surface on which to balance. Natural red features in the polished rock represent the female implicit in the male.

The Eternal Dance of Male and Female

Of all the cosmic dualities, gender is easily the most central to worshipers' own personal identities and the most commonly incorporated into tradition and myth. Almost all deities, for example, are designated either male or female and exhibit powers associated with masculinity or femininity. In some faiths, sacred objects of worship are directly inspired by male or female organs. Hindu devotees of Shiva, for instance, venerate phallic emblems called lingas *(left)*, which are often seated in concave objects called yonis that represent the vulva of a goddess. Geometric emblems like the Indian yantra above present the same duality in more esoteric form.

In religions that worship a male sky god and a female earth as depicted at right, fruitful harvests are often seen as the offspring of intercourse between the two. Similarly, human sexual union holds a mystical significance for many cultures, for it is in that energetic coupling of opposites that all future life — of either gender — begins.

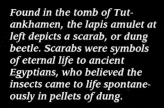

Found in the tomb of Tut-ankhamen, the lapis amulet at left depicts a scarab, or dung beetle. Scarabs were symbols of eternal life to ancient Egyptians, who believed the insects came to life spontaneously in pellets of dung.

Carved by an anonymous Celt around the second century BC, the warrior at right looks back to heroic feats and forward to his inescapable death. The Celts believed a fatalistic acceptance of death inspired greater courage in battle.

In a supposed case of natural resurrection, the legendary phoenix—pictured at right in a sixteenth-century German bestiary—was said to live 500 years, immolate itself on a pyre, then reappear in the ashes of its burned corpse.

Der Vogel Fenix.

Life and Death in an Endless Cycle

"Life follows upon death. Death is the beginning of life. Who knows when the end is reached?" wrote the fourth-century-BC Taoist Chuang Chou, who like most Eastern philosophers assumed human beings were reincarnated after death. "If then life and death are but consecutive states, what need have I to complain?"

As depicted in ageless images like the Celtic stone carving above, the human need to reconcile existing life with inevitable death—one's own, that of loved ones, even the autumnal death of vegetation and the waning of the winter sun—finds expression in every culture. Some religious faiths view death as final, with human identity surviving only in the memories of those left behind. But in other belief systems—from that of ancient Egypt to the Taoism of Chuang Chou, to mod-

ern Buddhism, Christianity, Islam, and the Hindu beliefs represented at right—death is not the end but the beginning of new life. Symbolizing the concept of rebirth through sacred images and fabulous tales, these traditions portray death as a doorway into another existence: in some faiths a paradise of eternal bliss or a hell of suffering, in others simply an opportunity to live another life on this earth.

The Hindu goddess Kālī stands over her consort Shiva's awakened persona while his double lies sleeping in this eighteenth-century painting. Worshiped as the source of both life and death, Kālī holds symbols of vitality—the lotus of regeneration and the bowl of abundance—in her left hands, while her right hands wield the sword and scissors of physical mortality. The goddess wears a necklace of severed human heads.

Ambivalent Symbols of Vice and Virtue

Just as any human being combines traits of both good and evil, so the recurrent symbols of human culture have often taken on a mixed significance, venerated in one era only to be despised in another. In ancient Greece, for example, most homes displayed paintings of beneficent snakes over the family altar. The snakes were considered symbols of earth magic, fertility, and regeneration. But in societies fearful of its sometimes deadly bite, the serpent became a guileful messenger of evil, typified by the Satanic specimen that tempted Eve in the Garden of Eden and brought about humankind's fall from grace.

Similarly, the unicorn with its thrusting horn seemed the embodiment of insatiable lust to many medieval European scholars. A twelfth-century rule book for nuns described the beast as wicked, wrathful, and an emblem for violent people, and a unicorn's horn soon came to be regarded as highly aphrodisiac. Yet the very pursuit of unicorn horns to make the treasured love potion led others to view the mythical beast as an innocent victim. In the traditions that shaped modern beliefs about the unicorn, trusting passivity came to the fore as the unicorn became the archetype of purity, virtue, and innocence betrayed.

A serpentine Hindu Naga guards the source of wisdom and sacred knowledge in the seventh-century Indian carving at upper left. Benevolent to the virtuous but capable of terrible violence against blasphemers, such serpent demigods were said to carry within themselves the forces of darkness and light, earth and water. To the ancient Egyptians, however, the serpent had no benevolent side. Every night, the snake demon, Apophis, spirit of darkness, attacked the sun god, Ra, seen here as a cat. As depicted in the fourteenth-century-BC painting from the Book of the Dead at left, Ra solved that problem by cutting off the demon's head.

In the sixteenth-century allegory above, a diminutive unicorn representing chastity peacefully rests its head on a maiden's lap. For much of recorded history, however, unicorns were more commonly viewed as muscular, lustful beasts with piercing horns. That perception of the creature holds full sway in Albrecht Dürer's 1516 engraving The Abduction of Proserpina (left), in which a unicorn, nostrils flared, hoofs pawing the earth, seems a willing accomplice to a forcible kidnapping.

CHAPTER 1

Dualities As Old As Time

he story was horrifying, bizarre, hair raising—and it so riveted moviegoers that by 1980 *The Exorcist* had rung up the fourth highest box-office receipts in motion-picture history. The film portrayed a case of diabolic possession, during which a little girl leads an appalling double life for a brief but terrifying period of weeks: One moment, she is a sugar-and-spice personification of good; the next, she has been transformed into a wicked, foul-mouthed embodiment of evil.

The grisly climax of the movie takes place in an elegant brick home in the fashionable Georgetown section of Washington, D.C. By the final reel, a wise old Roman Catholic priest has died of a heart attack, a young priest has leaped to his death from a window, and the innocent child whose body has been claimed by the demon is left curled on the floor, shriveled from malnutrition, but otherwise cured and utterly without memory of the horrifying acts to which she has been a party.

It is a short walk from the Key Bridge, which spans the Potomac River, to the narrow flight of stone stairs where the film crew of *The Exorcist* shot the pivotal scene in which the exorcist's assistant plunges to his death in a desperate attempt to banish the devil—the ultimate incarnation of evil. To this day, many Washingtonians quicken their pace as they pass that stairway, even though they doubtless realize that they have fallen victim to so much Hollywood trickery.

The plot of this box-office bonanza was in fact a highly fictionalized account of an actual case that involved an alleged demonic possession. In 1949, an exorcism was performed by Roman Catholic priests on a fourteen-year-old boy, whose sufferings had been formally recognized by the Church as the workings of Satan himself. The teenager's symptoms, however, were not of the same grotesque order as those wreaking havoc on the movie's tormented child, Regan MacNeill.

In the Hollywood version, Regan is afflicted with ghastly skin lesions and projectile vomiting. Her head is made to turn around on her neck a full 360 degrees, and her faculties and vocal cords are seized by the devil, who talks through her mouth in a child's sweet voice alternating with a frightful adult growl—or jabbers at length in Latin of things that a small girl could not possibly know.

Yet the symptoms of the real-life boy victim were strange enough in themselves. Welts reportedly appeared on his skin forming the words GO TO ST. LOUIS, and a variety of phenomena were said to have occurred in his presence that are most often associated with poltergeists. For one thing, the Lutheran pastor of the teenager's family church claimed to have seen the youngster's bed vibrating and its mattress undulating violently. The minister also spoke of having witnessed an episode in which the boy rose from the floor while seated in a chair and floated across the room. Some time later, after doctors had declared that the boy was perfectly normal, a Catholic priest who had been called in to assess the situation reported that a relic of Saint Mary Margaret had been torn from the bed and hurled against a mirror.

Eventually, a Catholic archbishop judged that the boy was diabolically possessed and authorized the performance of an exorcism. During the intensive campaign of prayer and religious devotion that followed—it lasted thirty-five days—the Jesuit priest undertaking the ritual waged a private war on Satan. The boy, meanwhile, suffered occasional convulsions and repeatedly lapsed into unconsciousness. He frequently shouted obscenities and lashed out violently with his fists, once breaking the nose of a seminarian who was assisting in the exorcism. Although the youngster knew no Latin, he uttered the word *Dominus* again and again. And he spoke of seeing a big red devil and nine smaller ones, who were driven away by Saint Michael the archangel. The "skin writing" phenomenon also recurred, climaxing—according to the

officiating priest, who took it as a sure sign of the devil at work—when the boy cried out the name of Jesus and marks appeared all over his chest forming the characters of the word HELL.

In due course, these strange occurrences came to an end, and the exorcism was pronounced a success. Happily, the boy's symptoms vanished and he went on to live a normal life. Yet ever since this episode transpired, some observers of religious matters have questioned whether the boy's sufferings were sufficiently grave to warrant a formal exorcism. The procedures in such cases are well established in Roman Catholic canon law, but many people felt that this poor tormented adolescent was racked by nothing more serious than extreme physiological disturbances brought about by the onset of puberty.

By the time these events had been fictionalized, however, and hyped up for use in a movie script, the audience was allowed little room for doubt concerning their gravity. The film conveyed the notion that the devil was clearly abroad, in full possession of a human soul, and nastily spoiling for a fight. On the screen, the young priest challenges the devil to enter his body instead of Regan MacNeill's and then sacrifices himself by plunging to his death in the hopes of taking Satan with him. Presumably, though, the Evil One manages to escape and continues his diabolic war on God and humanity.

What is certain is that Satan escaped into the public imagination. Obviously, the movie's lurid plot and sensational special effects accounted for much of its popularity, but it just as clearly struck a nerve for millions of viewers who found the subject matter terribly unsettling. Shortly after the film appeared in

1973, there was a sharp rise in the number of people claiming to be possessed by the devil—an increase noted both in the United States and abroad. Many troubled souls beseeched their ministers and churches to be granted rites of exorcism. Even people who were not so deeply confused by the message of the film felt jolted by reflections on the possibility of an evil force abiding in the world that competes with the forces of good for possession of human souls.

The compelling notion of an everlasting struggle between good and evil is as old as the history of human thought. It has figured in humankind's most ancient fantasies and has played a central role in many of the major religions. The philosophical and theological questions posed by the very existence of evil in the world continue to trouble many people to this day.

Yet the confrontation of good and evil is only one of myriad contrary elements in a universe apparently forged of paradox. From such earthly contrasts as day and night or male and female, to more abstract opposites such as love and hate or joy and sorrow, to life and death—the most profoundly disturbing disparity of all—the recognition of dualities, or opposing principles, at every turn in human existence has perplexed and haunted thinking people from time immemorial. It is not too broad a proposition to suggest that all of the myths, religions, and philosophies ever concocted have ripened from a deep-seated human need to explain the dualities inherent in the cosmos.

Proof of this age-old fascination with opposing forces is to be found in the legends that turn up in nearly every culture about a better place—an Eden, a heaven, or a nirvana—that was the original seat of human existence and must be our ultimate goal in this life. A consistent theme that crops up in all of these legends is that paradise is marked by a perfect unity: There, all is one; humans are united with the Divine and all dualities are eliminated, or at least rendered benign. Psychoanalyst Carl Jung described the concept of nirvana as a "liberation from opposites." In a related view, Rumanian-born religious scholar and historian Mircea Eli-

ade regarded paradise as a place where opposites could coexist without opposing each other. Eliade found in the mythologies of the world a great longing for a place where all contrary things could abide serenely together as part of a mysterious unity.

A vivid evocation of this ideal is presented in the great Islamic legend that describes the prophet Muhammad's night journey to the seven heavens of the universe. As Muhammad enters the second level of heaven, he encounters an angel of perfect beauty: "One half of his body was of ice and the other half of fire; and yet there was no counteraction nor enmity between them."

Thus one might imagine that a lonely shepherd in ancient Mesopotamia, being fearful of the cold and dark hours of the night, would naturally long for the comfort of daylight. He would yearn not so much for a world devoid of night, but for one in which the cold did not freeze his bones once the sun had departed and for one in which the darkness held no terrors.

Shepherds and princes alike knew all too well that the night was indeed fearsome. They also knew that human beings were just as capable of hating and fighting as of loving and cherishing one another, and that some babies sickened and died while others laughed and grew strong. It was probably inevitable, therefore, that people throughout the ages would continue to ask themselves what terrible things might have happened in that faraway paradise to upset its blissful unity and allow the ubiquitous effects of such monstrous contradictions. How had the world come so far from its pristine state of oneness?

Almost without exception, the world's great myths of creation undertake to answer this question by imagining a fall from the original state of oneness. As Eliade put it: "The world came into existence as a result of the breaking of primordial unity." The Fall, although it varied greatly in its innumerable versions in mythology, always sets loose a host of tribulations for the earth and its inhabitants. Yet the fall from grace or natural perfection is also understood to be an

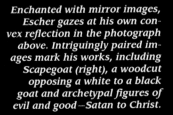

A Master Artist Who Tricks the Eye

"Isn't it fascinating to realize," wrote Dutch graphic artist Maurits Cornelis Escher *(left),* "that no image, no form, not even a shade or color, 'exists' on its own?" Instead everything visible, he said, depends on relationships and contrasts. Even black and white "only manifest themselves together and by means of each other."

In his mesmerizing prints—usually in white and black—Escher used paired opposites in pursuit of paradox and surprise. "We live," he insisted, "in a beautiful and orderly world, and not in a formless chaos, as it sometimes seems"—but "we adore chaos because we love to produce order."

Many of his intricate, beautifully ordered designs contain two opposed but simultaneously true realities: With an unexpected shift in the mind's eye, fish become sky and birds become water; up becomes down, and a finite square of paper displays an endless repetition. The artist called it "a pleasure knowingly to mix up two- and three-dimensionalities, flat and spatial, and to make fun of gravity."

Escher's body reflected his affinity for duality. Ambidextrous, he wrote with his right hand but drew with his left. And his work brought him another stark contrast—decades of poor earnings and obscurity, followed by twenty years of fame and wealth before his death, at seventy-four, in 1972.

Enchanted with mirror images, Escher gazes at his own convex reflection in the photograph above. Intriguingly paired images mark his works, including Scapegoat (right), a woodcut opposing a white to a black goat and archetypal figures of evil and good—Satan to Christ.

White angels and black batlike devils form one another's backdrops in Escher's Circle Limit IV (Heaven and Hell). "Good cannot exist without evil, and if one accepts the notion of God, one must postulate a devil likewise," the artist wrote.

Birds and fish meet and transform at the horizon in Escher's Sky and Water I; below the skyline, birds become sea, while above it, fish converge to form air. Escher noted that the eye cannot see the birds and the fish simultaneously but must focus on one at a time.

Scowling pessimists point cautiously at smiling, waving optimists in Escher's lithograph *Encounter*. Emerging from a flat, gray wall onto a three-dimensional, black-and-white stage, the figures seem to greet one another and shake hands.

At any corner of this popular Escher print, *Convex and Concave*, all seems normal, but when the eye crosses the center line, impossible contradictions intrude. Ascent becomes descent, floor becomes ceiling, and opposites somehow coexist.

essential prologue to the existence of humanity. As desirable as a state of perfect unity might be, it is also somehow beyond the bounds of the human imagination. Duality is not only inevitable, it seems; it is also entirely necessary. Eliade continues: "The world's existence, as well as existence in the world, presupposes a separation of light from darkness, a distinction between good and evil, a choice and a tension." Add to that list the distinction between male and female, and it would contain all the essential elements that are found in the myths of creation, stories that humans have spun out for thousands of years to explain their place in this fractured world.

In the earliest human cultures, formed as *Homo sapiens* emerged from the Stone Age, the earth itself was often perceived as a goddess, who was the original creator. Later cultures invented more elaborate religions and worshiped different gods, but the idea of the earth as a mother persisted in many of the legends about the world's creation. There is a glimpse of such a goddess in the mythology of the Pelasgians, a prehistoric people believed to have lived in what is now Greece before the rise of what is generally thought of as Western civilization.

In the beginning, according to the Pelasgian mythmakers, there was Chaos, which is where most creation stories originate. To the Pelasgians, however, Chaos was not just a great cloud of nothingness. Rather, it was a dynamic region that contained tremendous potential—a place of great energy but no differentiations to define things as separate or individual. There were, in short, no dualities. The grand scheme of creation, in this view, was to impose order on a limitless kernel of possibility. This idea was passed down through the centuries and has become part and parcel of our very definition of the universe: *Cosmos* is the Greek word for "order."

According to the Pelasgians, naked Eurynome, goddess of all things, was the first to arise from Chaos. From this and other clues, as a matter of fact, some historians have suggested that the Pelasgians probably lived in a ma-

triarchal society. In any event, Eurynome looked upon the vast sameness of Chaos and almost inadvertently created the first cosmic duality: Finding nothing to stand on, she separated the sea from the sky so that she could dance on the waves. This primal division of matter resulted in distinctions between air and water, up and down, wet and dry, and it came to be looked upon by the Pelasgians as the first step in bringing forth order from Chaos. Because there were now at least two separate principles, they believed, there would have to be interaction between the opposing forces, and this brought about the entire creation process.

Along with order would come trouble, however, and it is worth noting that the root of the German word for "sin" is *Sünde,* which is also related to a German word for "sever" or "separate." As Eurynome danced, she stirred up behind her the north wind, or Boreas, which she then transformed into a great serpent called Ophion. Eurynome's dance aroused the passion of Ophion, who wound himself around the body of the goddess and copulated with her. Becoming pregnant, Eurynome took the form of a dove and eventually laid the universal egg, which the serpent then wrapped in the coils of his body and held until it hatched. This act released all other things in the universe, and by this process, the sun, the moon, and all the heavenly bodies, including the earth, came into being.

If the separation of water and air embodies the first universal duality in the Pelasgian story of creation, the appearance of the serpent introduces another, for he becomes the masculine half of the male-female duality. The serpent would play this same role in many other creation myths as well. In this one he is dependent on the female force for his existence but is nevertheless necessary for the creation of the world. The wind god turned serpent is therefore a giver of life, and some scholars have connected Ophion to the old superstition that mares can become pregnant without making contact with a stallion simply by turning their hindquarters to the wind.

The Pelasgian myth goes on to relate that Eurynome

and Ophion settled down on Mount Olympus, where they lived until a ferocious domestic argument broke out. It seems that the serpent, rising above his station, began to claim that he, not she, actually created the universe. Furious, Eurynome kicked out the serpent's teeth and banished him to the underworld. For the human race this battle would have enormous consequences: From Ophion's teeth, Eurynome created the first man, Pelasgus, and originated the prehistoric race of Pelasgians.

Gradually the ancient matriarchal cultures (if in fact they ever actually existed; some scholars dismiss this interpretation of old myths) gave way to male-dominated ones, and the hierarchy of deities reflected the change. By the eighth century BC, when the Greek poet Hesiod's epic, *Theogony,* provided a genealogy for the already vibrant pantheon of Greek gods and goddesses, the Supreme Being was the male deity Zeus.

Yet Hesiod's story of creation, like that of the Pelasgians, begins with the female principle. According to Hesiod, Gaia—or earth—rose from Chaos to set in motion the entire process of creation. She bore a son, Uranus, who represented the star-filled heavens and thus was the opposite of his mother the earth. And Uranus came to equal his mother in grandeur.

In creating the duality of heaven and earth, Gaia imposed the beginnings of order on Chaos. Now it was time to people the universe, so Gaia and Uranus coupled and produced a divine race called the Titans. There were six female Titans and six male ones, as well as a later variety of monstrous beings known as Cyclopes. Once again, as in the Pelasgian myth, there was a falling-out between the earth goddess and her consort, because the hideous Cyclopes so horrified Uranus that he shut them up in a place far beneath the earth. So far below heaven was this place, in fact, that the myth says it took an anvil nine days of falling to reach its depths.

Uranus's act so enraged Gaia that she conspired with her last-born Titan son, Cronos, to punish her former partner. Cronos did so with a vengeance. Waiting until Uranus slept, the Titan seized his father's genitals, cut them off with a sickle provided by his mother, and threw them into the sea. From Uranus's awful wound the Furies were loosed, and out of subsequent conflicts among the Titans, Zeus was born to assume control of the universe and oversee the birth of humankind.

Although the details of these two creation stories differ, the myths are similar in that they both postulate that a primal separation—in the one case, the parting of the heavens and the seas, and in the other, the division of heaven and earth—is an essential condition for the creation of the physical world. Then in order to people the universe, first with gods and later with humans, both stories contrive to establish another fundamental dualism, that of female versus male. Neither myth, of course, provides any clue to the unanswerable question of what there was before Chaos came into being.

A strong theme of violence runs through most of the creation myths, and in many of them dismemberment of a god or primal being provides the substance for the next stage of generation. Thus Uranus was brutalized by his son Cronos, who is in turn eviscerated by his offspring Zeus. A powerful Babylonian myth describes how heaven and earth were fashioned from the body of a dragon called Tiamat, cut in two on the battlefield by the heroic warrior Marduk. According to the Maori of Polynesia, Tane-mahuta, son of Pangi the sky father and Papa the earth mother, had to rend his parents before he could emerge from the womb. In Norse mythology a huge hermaphroditic giant called Ymir is sundered by three of his grandsons. Then, as one version of the story recounts: "Of Ymir's flesh the earth was fashioned, / And of his sweat the sea; / Crags of his bones, trees of his hair, / And of his skull the sky."

Not all stories of creation were so rooted in violence, however. Around the time that Hesiod was living in Greece—most likely, the eighth century BC—Hindu priests in India were writing a series of poetic dialogues called the Upanishads, which were commentaries on the even more

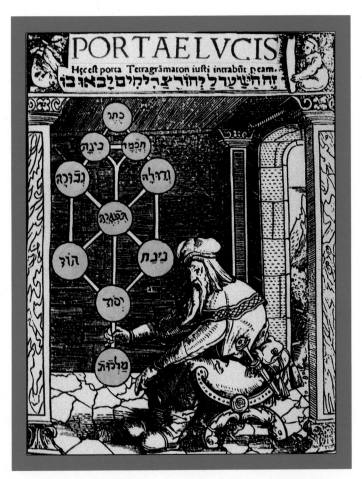

A Jewish cabalist holds the tree of life in this 1516 illustration. The spheres represent ten facets of God, including the opposing male on the right and female on the left and a harmonizing midline.

ty, this tale from the Upanishads also provided a motive for creation in the loneliness of the original being. This theme is reflected in several other creation myths as well. A Bulgarian legend, for example, tells how God was out walking alone one day when he spied his shadow following him. "Get up, comrade," God urged, and Satan emerged from the shadow requesting that the universe be divided equally between them. The two signed a contract to the effect that God would hold sway over the living, while Satan commanded the dead.

similar legend that originated in central Asia depicts God sitting on a rock wishing that he was not alone. "If only I had a brother, I would make the World," he says, and spits onto the waters. From his spittle a mountain takes shape before his eyes. When he splits the mountain with his sword, the devil steps out, asking to be his brother. God balks at such a relationship with the devil, but he does agree that they should become companions. Between the two of them, God and the devil create the world and fill it with many perplexing contradictions.

Creation myths helped ancient peoples feel as if they had some understanding of how the world got to be such an unharmonious place. In a similar fashion, one role of the world's multitude of religions—many of which grew out of their attendant myths—has been to rationalize life's ongoing dissonances. In early polytheistic religions, like those of ancient Greece and Rome, the pantheon of gods always included a number of bad actors or mischievous spirits who could be blamed whenever things went awry. However, when the uncompromisingly monotheistic creeds of Judaism, Christianity, and Islam evolved, life's troublesome dualities became harder to explain away. The problem is a thorny one: If God is all powerful and all good, how can he tolerate the existence of evil in the world?

There have been many answers proposed in response to this vexing riddle. Some religions, while maintaining God's omnipotence, insist that he allows evil to exist in or-

ancient writings called the Veda, the scriptures of the Hindu religion. One of these dialogues contains an account of how the Supreme Self, the deity sometimes called Brahma, went about the task of creating the cosmos in a much gentler and more generous way.

In the beginning this Self was alone, but because he was lonely, he took no delight in his existence. To remedy this situation, he made himself fall into two, and there arose a man and a woman to fill the void. These two embraced, thus establishing the human race. The original man and woman, born of the Supreme Self, went on to transform themselves by turn into a cow and a bull, a mare and a stallion, and so forth all the way down to the ants. And in this way all living creatures came into being. Brahma came to be regarded as a sort of all-in-one duality—the embodiment of diversity and, at the same time, the single Supreme Self in which everything was one.

Besides introducing the idea of a self-contained duali-

der to test the faith of his followers. Most Christian creeds teach that the whole matter boils down to the free will that is at the disposal of humanity. According to this line of argument, God created Satan so that the descendants of Adam would be forced to choose between the paths of righteousness and corruption. However much havoc the forces of evil might wreak, they will always be subordinate to the almighty force of Good. In a few cases, religions have faced the problem of evil head-on by adopting a position known in theological scholarship as dualism.

In reality, every religion incorporates certain aspects of dualism, because they all in one way or another distinguish between what they consider sacred and what they hold to be profane. Put more simply, they make a clear distinction between good and bad behavior. In precise theological terms, however, a religion that is truly dualistic postulates the coexistence of two fundamentally separate forces of good and evil. It teaches that these opposing forces will be eternally distinct and forever at odds with each other in the universe.

ne ancient creed that embraced such a concept was Zoroastrianism, which arose in Persia, long a meeting ground for ideas from both the Eastern and the Western worlds. Also known today as Parseeism, Zoroastrianism probably took shape around the sixth century BC. It is thought to have exerted a significant influence on later developments in both Judaism and Christianity, but it differed substantively from those religions in its insistence on the separateness of the two great principles of good and evil.

Zoroaster, the founder and prophet of this still-vigorous religion, is thought to have been born near Tehran, the capital of present-day Iran, about 600 years before the birth of Christ and twelve or so centuries before the birth of Muhammad, the prophet of Islam. Little is known about the details of Zoroaster's life, but legend suggests that his birth was a miraculous event.

A young woman named Dughdov conceived a child, but God intervened and the three parts of this child's be-ing—his heavenly glory, his guardian spirit, and his bodily self—passed through heaven and settled in the expectant mother's womb. Even before the birth, the story goes, Zoroaster's radiance was so great that his mother's body lighted up the whole of his father's village. Upon coming forth, the baby smiled and a light continued to surround the house. It was said that from the day of his birth he could communicate with God, who was known in ancient Persia as Ahura Mazda, or Ohrmazd.

Zoroaster grew up in spiritual bliss, and at about the age of thirty, he set off to wander in the desert for a period of meditation and soul-searching. There he had a vision in which he was transported into the presence of God, and from that time until his death at the age of seventy-seven, he devoted his life to converting the Persians to a new faith. In time, Zoroaster, who is also known as Zarathustra, came to be revered as a model for priests, warriors, and farmers. He was also esteemed as a great healer, a mathematician, and a scholar.

The earliest teachings of Zoroaster have survived in the form of seventeen hymns called the Gathas. These focused on Ohrmazd, the highest god, creator of heaven and earth, and on his fierce opponent, Ahriman, who was the spirit of evil. Surrounding Ohrmazd in his battle against Ahriman were embodiments of his noble attributes, among them truth and immortality. These qualities came to be identified with specific individuals, who were somewhat similar to the Christian archangels. They would be called Amesha Spentas, or Bounteous Immortals, by the Zoroastrians. Ranged against them, under the command of Ahriman, were vile demons and archdemons of which the most insidious was a personification of dishonesty known as Lie.

Zoroaster's cosmology was essentially monotheistic, because Ohrmazd was supreme. Yet Ohrmazd had not created Ahriman and did not entirely control him. The devil

In Rembrandt's 1638 etching Adam and Eve, the two huddle under the tree of knowledge and contemplate the forbidden fruit. In the Bible, the serpent urged Eve to taste the fruit, saying, "God knows that when you eat of it your eyes will be opened, and you will be like God, knowing good and evil."

had freely chosen his path of wickedness and was expected to pursue his evil ways right up to the bitter end. Ohrmazd would not prevail until sometime in the distant future. At that time all the world would be raised up to live with God in his glory.

The centuries that followed the life of Zoroaster added layers of myth and dogma to the master's teachings. Eventually, Ohrmazd was reduced to the level of Ahriman so that the two of them became coequal spirits, locked in eternal conflict. Here was a fully dualistic formula in which the god of good was in no way responsible for the presence or the power of evil. The separation of good and bad was so complete in this later form of Zoroastrianism that two distinct vocabularies were used in discussing them. Consequently, Zoroastrians reserved the words *head, hand, speaking,* and *dying* for use in reference to the forces of good, while using words such as *skull, claw, howling,* and *perishing* in talking about the evil forces.

This view of equally matched influences for good and for evil carried a certain element of fatalism, but Zoroastrianism remained somehow an essentially optimistic creed—indeed, it came to be known by its followers as the Good Religion. Zoroaster had taught that the physical world in all its manifestations was the creation of Ohrmazd and, therefore, of good, and that even though the flesh was subject to Ahriman's temptations, it could not in itself be evil. Asceticism and denial of the virtuous pleasures of life were regarded by Zoroaster as denials of God. On the day of the month dedicated to God, devout Zoroastrians were enjoined to ''drink wine and be merry.'' Courtesy and charity, along with a deep-seated respect for fellow creatures of nature, were other hallmarks of the religion.

The Good Religion became the official faith of the Persian Empire in the third century AD. But as might have been expected in the cauldron of religious foment and creativity that we now call the Middle East, there were disagreements among the different factions of Zoroastrianism that brought about schisms and sweeping reevaluations of many of the prophet Zoroaster's teachings. One religious movement that may have arisen as part of this splintering process was called Zurvanism. The origins of Zurvanism are not entirely clear, and it may have been a completely separate religion. If indeed it was an offshoot of Zoroastrianism, it greatly diluted the dualistic focus of the parent religion.

Zurvanism taught that a higher principle, thought of as Infinite Time, or Zurvan, gave birth to Ohrmazd and Ahriman, who were twins. Thus the opposing spirits of good and evil were no longer irreducible forces but the prod-

This Syrian fresco records a rare image of the Persian prophet Zoroaster, who taught, probably six centuries before the birth of Christ, that good can and must overcome evil.

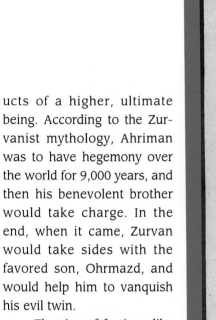

ucts of a higher, ultimate being. According to the Zurvanist mythology, Ahriman was to have hegemony over the world for 9,000 years, and then his benevolent brother would take charge. In the end, when it came, Zurvan would take sides with the favored son, Ohrmazd, and would help him to vanquish his evil twin.

The rise of factions like Zurvanism marked a period of decline for Zoroastrianism, but the end of that creed as a major world religion came in the seventh century AD, when the potent tide of Islam spread over Persia and the whole Middle East. The Good Religion is still practiced today by about 10,000 people in Iran, however, and by perhaps 100,000 or so Parsees of the Indian subcontinent, where some followers of Zoroaster resettled after being displaced by Islam.

A dictum familiar to some scholars of religious history instructs that orthodoxy breeds heresy. And just as Zurvanism probably sprouted among disgruntled Zoroastrians, so another mutinous doctrine grew in rebellion to Judaism, the still-new Christianity, and the religions of Persia. This doctrine came to be known as Gnosticism, from the Greek word *gnosis,* which means "knowledge." The ideas that the Gnostics embraced had nothing to do with intellectual or scientific learning but revolved around what one Gnostic tract called "knowledge of the heart." The Gnostics believed that truth came to them through personal revelation rather than through faith or liturgical instruction. This atti-

A copy of an ancient Persian work shows that Ohrmazd, Zoroastrian god of good (bottom, right), defeats his winged evil twin, Ahriman—if mortals (top) choose to do good.

tude was expressed in modern times by Carl Jung who, when asked if he believed in God, responded, "I don't need to believe, I know."

As Gnosticism grew in the shadow of the orthodox religions, it developed an inherently dualistic outlook on the world. In general, humankind was seen to possess a spark of divine goodness, sometimes called the pneuma, or breath. But the physical world itself was regarded as irrevocably evil. Thus, even the human body, which gave shelter to the pneuma, was considered profane, because it was part of the material world. Gnostics in the Jewish tradition saw the Hebrew God, Yahweh, as merely a lesser spirit, or demiurge, who had created the world and along with it death and everything evil.

Similarly, Christian Gnostics saw no good in the world, and no hope of salvation except through absolute denunciation of the flesh. In the view of one second-century Gnostic teacher, Christ never really became human, because he could not actually assume a physical body, which would by its nature be evil. What Christ did do, according to this view, was to show humanity that the way to communicate with the divine was through personal revelation.

The dualism of the Gnostics was gloomy in the extreme, because it had nothing but revulsion for the physical world. Followers of this tradition could still be found in the lands of the eastern Mediterranean as late as the sixth century, but the religion had ceased to be a serious threat to Christianity or Judaism by about AD 300. In all probability,

A wooden twin doll from West Africa's Hausa tribe depicts twins as both two beings and one. Some peoples, believing gods to be born in pairs, greet the birth of twins with joy; others see twins as evil and on their birth perform rituals to ward off misfortune.

the teachings of Gnosticism were both too hostile and too esoteric ever to have formed the basis for a broad-based, popular religious movement. And the fledgling Catholic church may have usurped whatever appeal Gnosticism did hold by incorporating its concerns into the still-formative Christian theology. Nevertheless, in the fourth century, the Catholic hierarchy pronounced Gnosticism an apostasy and took steps to eradicate it as a formal religion by means of severe persecution.

Gnosticism never completely died out, however, and it inspired several subsequent dualistic religious movements. In the third century BC, Gnostic influences helped give shape to Manicheanism, which is often seen as the quintessentially dualistic religion. Manicheanism was founded by the son of a noble family named Mani, who was born in the year 216 near Seleucia-Ctesiphon, the capital of the Persian Empire. At age twelve, according to legend, Mani was visited by an angel called at-Taum, after the Persian word for "twin." This spirit was sent by God to command the boy to leave his father's religious sect, which combined Gnostic, Jewish, and Christian religious precepts. Twelve years later, at-Taum confronted Mani once again, instructing him to go forth and proclaim his own doctrines. From that moment on, the angel became Mani's spiritual twin and accompanied him in all his travels, guiding him and inspiring him right up to the religious leader's death, when at-Taum opened the gate to heaven.

During his life, Mani journeyed widely throughout Persia and for a time was exiled to India. He claimed that his preaching fulfilled the work of Zoroaster, Jesus, and Buddha, all of whose teachings he had studied and mastered. But Mani seemed most driven by his hatred for the notion that God could possibly have created evil. Rejecting that idea, he proposed a rather complex religious mythology that expanded on the premises of Gnostic dualism. He postulated that there were two fundamental principles from the beginning: God, who is greatness and light, and Hylé, who is inherent in all earthly matter and is an equal to God in terms of power. The physical world had been created from the bodies of Hylé's followers. They had imprisoned the spark of divine light in the gross materials of plants, animals, and human beings in order to protect it. Mani repudiated the Christian sacraments, believing that only knowledge could save one's soul and that no mere ritual could cleanse the flesh of its inherent evil.

The founder of Manicheanism preached that the best hope for preserving and liberating the divine spark was to purify it through a life of asceticism. Only by denying the flesh, he believed, could one gain a true knowledge of one's self and thereby find a means to communicate with God, as he had managed to do with the help of his angelic twin. Mani prescribed a life of rigid self-denial in which the elect of his disciples were required, among other things, to forgo material wealth, sexual intercourse, and any more than one vegetarian meal a day. Devotees who were not prepared to undertake such puritanical measures were referred to as "hearers," and they could serve God by providing food and other necessities for those who had chosen the strait-laced path of self-denial.

Mani predicted that when the end of the world came, all those who had struggled to keep the divine spark alive would be relieved of their material baggage and elevated to the sphere of eternal light. Sinners and the world's physical dross would then be squeezed into a great round lump of filth, called the *globus,* and banished forever to the realm of darkness. The inherent dualism of the cosmos would thus be perpetuated for all eternity.

Mani was imprisoned by the Persian ruler Bahram I, who considered him a threat to the Zoroastrian faith. The religious leader died in chains in the year 276; his body was flayed and the skin stuffed with straw to be displayed for all to see. The religion he left behind combined features of Christianity, Buddhism, and Zoroastrianism, as well as elements of Hindu devotion. Despite the extraordinary demands that it placed on adherents, it found ready acceptance in many regions from China to Rome.

Manicheanism survived as a major Asian religion for

nearly a thousand years. In the West, its influence was considerable, but much more short-lived. In the fifth century, the great champion of Catholic orthodoxy, who would eventually be canonized as Saint Augustine, was a Manichean for nine years before converting to the Roman church and seeking his salvation through baptism. Like the teachings of Gnosticism, however, Manicheanism eventually ran afoul of Roman Catholicism, which branded it heretical. And by AD 600, Manicheanism, too, had been eradicated as a formal religion in the West.

The essence of Mani's message surfaced again in the teachings of a tenth-century Bulgarian priest named Bogomil. He also believed that all material things were evil and filthy. They were the work of the devil, whom Bogomil claimed to be the elder son of God and the brother of Christ. Despite this relationship, Bogomil held that the works of Satanael, as he called the devil, were absolutely distinct from the spiritual universe of God. The manifestation of Christ on earth and his Crucifixion were seen by Bogomil as mere illusions. The Bulgarian's followers, who themselves came to be known as Bogomils, taught that the Virgin Mary had not actually given birth to Christ but that he had entered her body through her right ear and then issued forth again as a phantom. Even the cross on which Christ had been killed was to be reviled according to the Bogomils, because it had been made by Satanael.

Marriage and procreation, which could lead only to the production of yet more matter, were abhorred within this view, along with meat, wine, churches, and any form of church hierarchy. The Bogomils rejected the sacrament of baptism and denied the presence of Christ in the eucharist. The only set way for devout followers to express their faith was by reciting the Lord's Prayer at regular intervals night and day.

This bare-bones version of Christianity somehow found fertile ground in Bulgaria and Asia Minor and even flourished for a while among the aristocracy of Constantinople. It was finally suppressed by the Otto-man Turks in the fourteenth century. By that time, the word *Bogomil* had come to denote anyone who espoused outlandish beliefs. Another brief but stark reemergence of the influences of Manicheanism occurred in southern France and northern Italy in the twelfth and thirteenth centuries. Called Catharism, it apparently arrived via Asia, inspired by Byzantine Gnosticism in addition to Manicheanism, and probably by the ideas of the Bogomils as well. Because of their uncompromising views on the proper standards for piety, chastity, and poverty, the Cathars believed that they were closer to the spirit of true Christianity than were the followers of the Roman Catholic church. The name given to their doctrine was derived from the Greek word *katharos,* which means ''pure.''

For the Cathars, evil was considered a primal, eternal element that was separate in every way from God's spiritual realm. Satan, who was the chief promulgator of evil, was not as powerful as God. But God was not so mighty as to be able to prevent Satan from creating the material world, which was held to be wicked and transitory. The Cathars believed that even if the earth should someday vanish, by some unforeseen turn of events, evil would remain in existence. The way to salvation, according to this sect, was through a life of self-denial and religious ritual calculated to promote firsthand encounters with the Divinity through direct psychic contact.

Like the Manicheans and the Bogomils, the Cathars felt that human beings could become worthy of such divine illumination only by denying the flesh that imprisoned their souls. Total abstinence from animal flesh, strong drink, sex, or any sort of creature comfort was the lifelong regimen of the most devout Cathars, who were known within the sect as "the Perfect." Barefoot and plainly dressed, pale and thin from fasting, these holy men walked from village to village, preaching a return to the true Church of Christ and condemning the rituals and excesses of the Church of Rome. In many places, the message of the wandering Cathar ascetics was eagerly received by a populace that was anxious for spiritual revival.

Like other austere dualistic creeds, the Cathars were careful to accommodate those listeners who were attracted to their message but not willing to adopt the severe lifestyle of the Perfect. Such run-of-the-mill "believers" came to make up the great majority of Cathar faithful and were allowed to lead more or less normal lives. By the middle of the twelfth century, they had become so numerous, particularly in the Languedoc region of south-central France, that the cathedrals of the Roman Catholic church were looking noticeably empty during mass. Faced with this severe challenge, the hierarchy of the Church of Rome once again raised the red flag of heresy and responded with brute force. In 1208, Pope Innocent III proclaimed a crusade against the Cathars, launching one of the most vicious assaults in the long history of religious conflict.

A series of military crusades, led by greedy nobles from the north of France under the banner of the Church of Rome, ravaged the southern regions of that country with unprecedented ferocity. In 1209, for example, the entire town of Béziers, a Cathar stronghold, was destroyed and its 20,000 citizens were put to death at the order of the Catholic bishop of Cîteaux. In 1244, the last open resistance of the Cathars was crushed when the crusaders sacked the town of Montségur and burned 200 of the Perfect. By that time, more than a million people had been slaughtered in this horrifying campaign, and by the mid-fourteenth century, the Cathar heresy had been exterminated. The Church fathers in Rome could breathe easily again.

Most historians believe that the religious issues were little more than a pretext for an out and out land grab by the powerful aristocrats who led the crusade against the Cathars. For at least some within the Church hierarchy, however, the religious disputes were very significant indeed. At the heart of the disagreement was the dualistic conviction on the part of the Cathars that all matter was inherently evil. From this perspective, Christ the Savior could not possibly have been born of the flesh of Mary, and his corporeality could only be understood as an illusion. Furthermore, Christ's death on the cross would have to be a fiction, and his physical resurrection would run counter to logic. After all, the highest objective from the Cathars' point of view was to shuck the body altogether and achieve a purely spiritual existence.

The denial of God's supremacy over evil struck at the heart of Roman Catholic doctrine, which held that by bringing together the spirit and the flesh in the person of Jesus, God had resolved the duality posed by the coexistence of good and evil. In this supreme gesture, God had demonstrated that the weaknesses of the flesh could be transcended by purity of spirit. Not only could the human flesh be cleansed, but the devil himself could be neutralized by earnest evocation of the Word of the Lord. It is to this optimistic end that the ritual of exorcism is invoked in doing battle with Satan when

Surprise waits within a painted wooden thunderbird mask (left), which yawns open (right) to reveal a human face. Members of the Haida and other tribes of the Northwest Coast wore such masks during ritual dances, acting out their belief in the dual human and animal nature of their gods.

he has succeeded in taking possession of a human soul.

For the short term, the Catholic church succeeded in suppressing the dualistic heresies that threatened its supremacy over Western religious expression. But awareness of the dualities that are implicit in human existence would never disappear altogether. The idea was lodged too firmly in the secular philosophies of the West and had been since long before the birth of Christ. For their part, the philosophies of the East tended to take a much less hard-edged view on this matter—in fact, they often embraced the essential dualities.

One of the earliest explicitly dualistic philosophies to find expression in the West was enunciated by the Pythagoreans in the sixth or fifth century BC. These Greek thinkers, who were of a mathematical bent, set out to describe the world with what might today be viewed as scientific objectivity. But what they actually described was a world permeated by contradictory forces. According to their intellectual descendant, Aristotle, the Pythagoreans discerned ten first principles of the world, set out in a list of opposites. The opposing principles were limited and unlimited, odd and even, square and oblong, at rest and in motion, straight and crooked, one and plurality, right and left, light and darkness, male and female, and good and evil.

Such rational binary exposition set the stage for the philosopher Plato, who was born in Athens in 427 BC and studied at the foot of Socrates. Plato went beyond the explicit dualities expressed in the Pythagoreans' list of opposites and suggested that form has an altogether separate existence from matter. He taught that every material thing has a corresponding ideal form that is distinct from the object itself. Within this scheme, physical objects are subject to change and decay, but their ideal form—their idea—is eternal and unchanging. Thus humans may be different from one to the next, and are certainly mutable and temporary, yet they have an ideal, immutable form that is humanity itself. Plato's concept of dualism applied as well to abstract ideas as it did to physical objects. For example, an object could be beautiful, whereas quite apart from the particular qualities of that object was an ideal form that might be dubbed ''beauty itself.''

Plato believed that ideal form or true reality could be comprehended by the intellect only in its function of exercising reason. On the other hand, the ephemeral reality of material things was the province of the senses. In thus elevating the intellect above sensual perception, Plato glorified reason as the highest component of the human psyche and credited logic with being the sole path to the perception of ideal reality. His eloquent arguments proving the separation of intellect from feeling have resonated persuasively throughout the history of Western theology and philosophy. It can even be argued that his ideas were at the root of an implacable dualism that, more than a thousand years later, gave rise to modern scientific thinking.

The Greek philosopher's vision of the structure of the universe was of tremendous significance and is a prime example of a particular way humans have dealt with the problem of duality. Twentieth-century American philosopher Alan Watts has written that the human mind tends to reduce things to binary comparisons and finds it easier to think in terms of either and or than of both and and. In the same vein, Carl Jung attested that "the essence of the conscious mind is discrimination; it must, if it is to be aware of things, separate the opposites." Such views suggest an explanation for the philosophical outlook that tries always to perceive the world in terms of hard-edged dichotomies—everything must be either this or that. Such a mental approach has been particularly evident in the philosophies of the Western world.

Many religions and philosophies, however, particularly in the East, have taken a more supple approach to duality. While recognizing the ubiquity of opposites in the world, these viewpoints tend to describe the opposites in terms of polarity rather than duality. Within such an approach, paired disparities are regarded as two parts of the same whole rather than as antagonistic dichotomies. For example, if birth is viewed as implying death, then death might logically imply rebirth.

The word *polarity* is derived from the Greek word *polos*, which means "pivot." A magnet provides an example in the physical world of the somewhat elusive Eastern understanding of duality: It is a bit of metal that contains two poles of force—positive and negative—that are nevertheless totally interdependent. A magnet without its two polar forces is nothing more than a lump of metal.

Perhaps the most evocative representation of polarity is the yin-yang symbol commonly associated with Chinese religion and philosophy. The symbol is a circle that is half black and half white, the two halves separated by a sigmoid line, curving in two directions like the letter *s*. Thus each side of the symbol demonstrably penetrates the other and contains a seed of the other. The light half, yang, is thought of as the active side and is associated with the male principle and heaven. The dark half, on the other hand, is considered passive and is associated with the female principle and earth. Always, however, these dualities are joined inseparably and together form the whole.

According to an ancient Chinese text known as the *I Ching*, or *Book of Changes*, these complementary opposites sprang from a single cosmic cell, called *ch'i*, or *qi*, which was brought into existence by the creative force called Tao. Out of the continuing creativity of Tao, the dualities produced everything else. This process of creation represented a dynamic system in which everything was in a state of continual flux and invention. The goal—implicit in the yin-yang symbol—was to achieve harmony between fluctuating states of oppositeness.

In a similar fashion, two of the great religions of the East, Hinduism and Buddhism, stress the interconnectedness of life's dualities instead of their separateness. For example, one of Hinduism's most important mythical figures is Shiva, who is both the god of creation and of destruction. Shiva is also identified with the masculine principle; his opposite is the goddess Shakti. In a culture whose mythology is rich in erotic anecdote and symbolism, the male-female duality is recognized explicitly, and yet the merging of the sexes is far more important than their differences. The importance of the union of Shiva and Shakti is honored in the saying, "Shiva without Shakti is a corpse." Indeed, Tantra—one of the many different strands of Hinduism—teaches that salvation can be achieved by the ritualized endeavor to achieve perfect sexual union.

Although Hinduism and Buddhism recognize humanity's sense of separation from cosmic unity, both religions hold that the perception of

Fortuna, the four-handed Roman goddess of destiny, mocks free will as she forces humans to ride the wheel of fortune—a device that allots good and bad luck by chance alone.

Facing both sun and moon, the two-headed dragon (right) was for alchemists a symbol of the dual nature of mercury—both metal and liquid. As the scientist-spiritualists of the Middle Ages, alchemists sought to transform metal into gold and also to raise their own earthly impurity to golden perfection. They symbolized the reconciliation of opposites, as in the hermaphrodite Rebus (below) and in the marriage of sun and moon (opposite).

---

being apart is in fact an illusion. In the Vedanta philosophy of Hinduism, the unity of the self with the whole is considered an eternal reality. It is not part of some distant nirvana; rather, it exists in the present. Thus, the goal for humanity is not to achieve union but simply to recognize it and embrace it.

In the same vein, Buddhism teaches that humans bring upon themselves anxieties over their perceived duality, because they fail to understand that all dualities are in fact part of the whole. They also invent a false "I," or ego, that is perceived as being separate from the rest of the universe. A key element in Buddhist practice is the struggle to achieve samadhi, a mystical state in which the believer is able, through a rigorous course of meditation, to rise above all the perceived dualities and to resolve all the conflicts within his or her body and spirit.

Many other branches of Eastern thought and religion have taken similar steps in stressing the importance of reconciling dualities rather than simply dwelling on them. Two such practices that found their way to the West in ancient times were astrology and alchemy. Both were to some degree forerunners of modern scientific disciplines—astrology predated astronomy, and alchemy was an early form of chemistry. Likewise, both pursuits flourished throughout the Middle Ages in Europe, when spiritual and mystical values were given precedence over the cold-eyed reason of the Greek philosophers.

Astrology has been described as one of the oldest attempts to find an answer to life's distressing dualities. From the beginning, humans must have noticed the apparent dichotomy between the earth and the heavens: All around them, they perceived disorder—pestilence, war, unbridled emotion, unexplainable natural disasters—while in the night sky a cool harmony prevailed, guiding the stars and the planets. With the exception of the occasional comet or supernova explosion, events in the heavens seemed utterly regular and predictable. Surely, it seemed, celestial serenity must hold a message for those dwelling in the disorder below.

For millennia humans have tried to decipher that message, and in ancient cultures, those who could read the future in the motion of the planets were the most respected of seers. In the scientific climate of today's world, particularly in the West, the influence of astrology has been greatly diminished. But the sense that celestial forces must in some way influence terrestrial events has never died away, and books and articles providing horoscopes remain ubiquitous in many parts of the world.

Modern astrology focuses on the interplay of polarized cosmic energies as a guide to understanding the human condition. Astrologer Dane Rudhyar suggests that two universal energies, which he calls day-force and night-force, actively affect the dual roles that people are required to play as individuals and members of a society. Day-force represents the personal "I," while night-force signifies the collective "we." Between them, in constant but shifting balance as the seasons vary in their ceaseless cycle, the dual cosmic forces come together in a dynamic union of opposites that integrates the human urge for inner order, or personality, with the collective demands of social and cultural harmony.

The ancient art of alchemy was based on a belief in the unity of the universe and the relatedness of all material phenomena. To be sure, alchemy was a metallurgical craft, and alchemists toiled for centuries in their laboratories in a vain quest to turn base metals into gold. But alchemists were also philosophers, and their chemical theories and experiments were based on a commonly shared understanding of the nature of the physical world. Indeed, alchemy has come to be seen by some historians as a relatively coherent philosophical attempt to reconcile the dualities of the world and the human psyche, and—in particular—the duality of spirit and matter.

Most alchemists did not view good and evil with the inexorable dualism of the Gnostics, but they did believe that all earthly things, animate and inanimate, possessed a cosmic spirit. Within this framework, even metal was regarded as being somehow alive, to be purified and perfected in the same way that people could improve themselves. To the alchemists, the spirit of gold—which was clearly the highest form of metal—was simply imprisoned in the lesser metals, owing to some improper balance of mercury and sulfur or salt, the fundamental ingredients of all matter. Thus, the metals could aspire to higher spiritual states as easily as humans could. The process would occur at its own pace in nature, but the alchemist hoped to hurry it along. To elevate the base metals to their perfection as gold, the alchemists used a marvelous array of chemical processes designed first to reduce the metals to their fundamental ingredients and then to re-create or re-crystallize them into a new, more noble pattern.

In the same way, some alchemists aspired to guide the human spirit to a higher plane of oneness with the cosmic spirit. This transmutation of the psyche required intense, lifelong study and disciplined intellectual pursuit. The ultimate goal was to dissolve one's temporal identity and reshape it in a more perfect state, closer to one's true nature. In short, the goal was nothing less than spiritual salvation.

For European alchemists, eternal salvation was officially the business of the Catholic church. Perhaps for this reason, the alchemists' findings were often couched in mystifyingly allegorical terms. Still, it was not the Church that ultimately forced either the alchemists or the astrologers to go underground. What made their arts no longer tenable was the rise of a mechanistic view of the world that grew out of the reemergence of Plato's notions about the preeminence of reason over intuition. And a revolution in the sciences that began with the observation of Nicholas Copernicus that the heavens did not revolve around the earth further undermined the reputation of the magical arts.

The man who established Cartesian dualism, the seminal modern philosophy that gave rise to this new order, was a product of the Renaissance—a time that transformed many Western attitudes about society, aesthetics, and politics. René Descartes was born in France in 1596. A mathematician and philosopher who contributed to many areas of human learning, his most lasting legacy was to unshackle the scientific outlook from earlier preconceptions about the physical world, so that scholars could conceptualize entirely new theoretical models and mathematical laws.

Descartes conceived his thesis at the age of twenty-three, after a period of intense study that left him in a sort of creative frenzy. He considered the night of November 10, 1619, to be the turning point in his life; historians have called it the "pentecost of reason." That night, in the city of Ulm in Baden-Württemburg, Descartes had three separate but related dreams: In the first dream, he encountered horrifying phantoms in the street; in the second, he heard a deafening clap of thunder; and in the third dream, he read a mysterious book of poetry. Even Descartes had a hard time explaining the relevance of these dreams to the new system of thought he would propose, but it was clear to him that they represented a kind of elegy. To Descartes, his dreams signified a leave-taking from the "poetic" way of knowing that had characterized the philosophies of the Middle Ages. In those times, scholars had relied on an intuitive path to learning about the universe by being at one with it.

In the Cartesian era, intuition would take a back seat to reason, and scholars would begin to view humankind as separated from the rest of the cosmos. Descartes regarded the universe as being divided into *res cogitans* and *res extensa:* The former were all things conceived by the intellect, which could have no physical measurements; the latter were the things of the material world, which were measur-

able and could have no psychic component. The human body and the brain belonged to the second category, but the mind, along with its thoughts and desires, was res cogitans. Like Plato, Descartes felt that the res extensa were subject to change and decay and were therefore not beyond question or doubt. Only pure thought was absolute and indubitable—a conviction that led to Descartes's famous axiom, "I think, therefore I am."

Descartes's separation of thought from things led to a degree of philosophical objectivity that made it possible to devise abstract mathematical laws and to define the mechanical principles governing the physical workings of nature. In the earlier world-view, scholars perceived themselves as being one with nature to such a degree that they were essentially no different from a tree, for example, and thus were not truly open to the idea of analyzing the tree's precise physical structure. Only through detachment came objectivity. And with objectivity came a scientific understanding of the workings of the universe. Descartes acknowledged an omnipotent God, but he felt that all physical phenomena could be examined and explained in mechanical and mathematical terms. This insight led directly to the stunning scientific achievements of Isaac Newton and others a mere half-century later.

Yet Descartes's notion of mind and matter as utterly distinct, important as it was to the cause of scientific objectivity, led to some difficult paradoxes of its own. If the mind (res cogitans) and the brain (res extensa) operate independently, as Descartes maintained, then how can one explain the way that the mind seems to exert a direct causal influence over the body? If a person thinks about lifting his or her arm, and the arm rises, that should prove a causal connection betwen mind and matter. Descartes was confronted with this problem and never managed to frame a

A young woman, half her body a skeleton, embodies the ultimate duality as she gazes from The Mirror of Life and Death. This seventeenth-century French engraving belongs to a genre of art showing the ravages of time. The verse advises, "To love beauty is unwise, for time destroys it. In this world nothing lasts, everything changes, and the moment we start to live, we start to die."

LE MIROIR DE LA VIE, ET DE LA MORT

Mondains qui faictes cas des beautez d'un visage,
Scachez que les aymer, ce n'est pas estre sage,
Puis que le temps enfin les doibt faire perir,
Nous n'auons icy bas chose aucune asseurée,
Tout change et nostre vie a si peu de durée,
Qu'en commencent à viure on commence à mourir,

very satisfactory explanation. But his Dutch disciple, Arnold Geulincx, had an ingenious—if not altogether convincing—solution to the paradox.

Imagine two clocks, Geulincx suggested, which both keep perfect time. When one clock points to the hour, the chimes on the other one will always sound. Although it might seem that the one timepiece is causing the other to chime, they are in fact acting separately—only in perfect harmony. It may follow, Geulincx claimed, that the mind and the body just appear to be working together: When the mind decides to raise the arm, the body lifts the limb, not because the mind has told it to do so, but because they are two perfectly synchronized organisms set in motion by God the clockmaker.

By the nineteenth century, Descartes's separation of mind and matter had led some philosophers to a perception of the world as a huge, soulless machine in which the spiritual aspirations of human beings were entirely subordinated to the mechanistic workings of governments and social classes. The most profound and influential statement of such an outlook took shape in the writings of Karl Marx and Friedrich Engels, lifelong friends and collaborators. The goal of these two political theorists was not only to explain but to eliminate what they considered to be an inevitable conflict between individuals and the larger society brought about by the enormous advances in technology during the Industrial Revolution.

The philosophy of Marx and Engels was called dialectical materialism: It was based on philosophical materialism and was "dialectical" to the extent that it relied on a method of logic popularized by philosopher Georg Wilhelm Friedrich Hegel in which the contradictions of opposing forces are continually resolved. Marx believed that all processes occurring in nature, philosophy, or human history were dialectical. The world was constantly changing, moving toward a perfect unity through a process in which opposites always came into conflict. The opposition of a thesis and an antithesis would eventually be resolved through a synthesis, but that resolution could result only in further conflict—until, that is, perfection was reached and the individual and society could exist in perfect harmony.

In historical terms, Marx and Engels believed that the bourgeois revolution would arise from economic conditions brought about by the rise of industry. Capitalist expansion had created a class of wage slaves, called the proletariat, which was destined to revolt against the bourgeois society. This synthesis would eventually cause the destruction of both the bourgeoisie and the proletariat; then there would be a utopia in which there was no opposition between the individual and society.

Thwarting this desirable goal, said Marx, was human cupidity, which at least one writer has likened to Zoroastrianism's evil spirit, Ahriman. Greed would obstruct the historical path to utopia just as Ahriman would constantly throw himself in conflict with the goals of Ohrmazd. According to Marx, private property was the antithesis of the proletariat, and the proletariat would eventually be forced to abolish itself and wealth together. Marx reasoned that if the state took control of private property and seized the sources of capital in trust for society, the social class divisions would disappear. Individual wealth and the proletariat were opposites, he argued, and by eliminating the duality between them—that is, by distributing the wealth among the proletariat—society would achieve wholeness.

But it must seem to some Marxists that their grand scheme underestimated the power of Ahriman—or human cupidity—and, just as in Zoroastrian myth, the forces of opposition continue to blight humankind: Marxism, as it has been applied in the real world, has been blighted by human error. Karl Marx's notion for resolving social dualities and thus curing all social ills has faded with the gradual disintegration of Communist systems of government. Meanwhile, the social conflicts that first drew Marx's attention resurface as new political expressions of the ancient universal duality—developed nations against undeveloped nations, northern peoples versus those of the south. And so the world remains in the grip of the same familiar tension as humankind continues its age-old search for wholeness.

The Dark Side of Fairy Tales

Once upon a time, a boy climbed a beanstalk to a giant's castle, a fairy godmother rescued a girl from her wicked stepmother, and an ugly beast courted and won a beautiful maiden. In the enchanted world of fairy tales and nursery rhymes, such exotic goings-on are not only possible but commonplace. Talking wolves, child-devouring witches, and shape-shifting princes are run-of-the-mill characters in this mythical realm. On casual consideration, their adventures seem extraordinary, utterly remote from everyday life—but, in fact, the symbolism of these characters and events is highly relevant to the real world.

Such children's tales retain their appeal chiefly because they are fun and imaginative. But psychologists and others believe the stories work on a deeper level as well, symbolically mirroring important junctures in a child's development and evoking the fundamental dualities of good and evil, youth and maturity, or ignorance and enlightenment. Stories such as *Cinderella* and *Jack and the Beanstalk* speak from a timeless, placeless world in which universal themes defy barriers of culture, language, or era. Readers and listeners of all nationalities immediately recognize the archetypes featured in these tales: Witches and ogres, for instance, clearly caricature the evil in humankind, while beneficent fairies personify the good. The following pages examine six familiar stories that capture a few of the complexities of the human condition.

Secrets from a Child's Unconscious

In the human psyche, a ceaseless tug of war is played out between the forces of the conscious and unconscious mind. Children's stories illustrate this tension with characters symbolically confronting aspects of their personalities that were previously beyond their awareness. Such moments of self-recognition often yield surprising insights: As with real-life children, traits opposite those displayed on the surface dwell undetected in characters' unconscious thought processes.

In the nursery rhyme *Little Miss Muffet*, a girl is confronted in a startling manner by a symbol, psychologists would say, of her unconscious. Sitting calmly on a tuffet of earth, spooning up her bland repast of curds and whey, the girl is the epitome of childhood innocence and placidity. But with the arrival of the spider, the peaceful image explodes. The big, black, hairy insect—Little Miss Muffet's exact opposite—is what psychiatrist Carl Jung would call an example of the shadow archetype: an obscure and generally unexpressed

side of the child's own character. Miss Muffet's shadow manifests a dark and disturbing facet of her psyche—the evil that lurks within her.

Jack and the Beanstalk reveals that the unconscious can also house wondrous treasures. The story's hero at first seems more of an antihero. Having squandered his mother's limited resources, Jack rashly trades her last possession—a cow—for a few paltry beans. But the barter turns out to be a terrific bargain when the beans produce a lofty beanstalk, the boy's ladder to a brighter future. He climbs the amazing vine and raids the giant's treasure-filled castle, and the stolen goods provide wealth enough to ensure lifelong comfort for him and his mother.

On the literal level, this tale apparently condones theft. Symbolically, though, the stealing can be understood as Jack's discovery of the riches of his unconscious mind. The gifts he carries back home—a hen that lays golden eggs, bags of gold and silver, and a magical harp—are all metaphors for talents and abilities that formerly lay idle and unrecognized within him. Conscripting them into his service, he is transformed from a ne'er-do-well lad into a successful adult.

Imaginary Roles for Real Parents

Stepmothers, godmothers, and even motherly fairies often take the place of biological parents in children's stories. These substitutes are purely symbolic, for they represent the opposing qualities found in all parents.

In *Cinderella,* the kind fairy godmother and the wicked stepmother split between them the good and bad traits of a parent. The death of Cinderella's biological mother, which leaves the girl in the care of these antithetic surrogates, can be seen as an allegory depicting the inevitable end to a child's unquestioning belief in her mother's perfection.

Psychoanalyst Bruno Bettelheim wrote a book about fairy tales in which he told of an actual little girl who, upon realizing brokenheartedly that her mother sometimes got cross or even angry, fantasized that a cruel Martian had taken over her parent's body. The girl simply could not bear to believe that her beloved mother would behave so incongruously. Similarly, children hearing the tale of Cinderella are

likely to seize upon the evil stepmother as their scapegoat while embracing the fairy godmother as an example of the idealized perfect parent. By providing a mother figure thus neatly divided into her two separate aspects, the story gives children a rare opportunity to hate the bad in their parents without remorse and to love the good without hesitation.

The heroine of the story *Rapunzel* is relinquished at birth to the care of an enchantress. The girl flourishes in this nurturing household until she is twelve years old—significant as the approximate age of sexual maturity. Then the guard-

ian's love takes an unfortunate turn as she grieves over the prospect of Rapunzel's coming of age and leaving home to marry. To prevent such a separation, she locks the girl in a tower. When a young prince arrives to free the maiden, Rapunzel is delighted, eager for a new life as an adult. But the enchantress resorts to even greater cruelty, and the girl is forced to struggle for her independence before she can achieve lasting happiness. Children hearing the story get a glimmering of the emotional ambivalence that affects many parents as their sons and daughters learn to assert themselves as individuals.

Innocence at War with Experience

"Beauty very civilly thanked them that courted her, and told them she was too young yet to marry, but chose to stay with her father a few years longer." Numerous authorities have interpreted the heroine's demurrals in *Beauty and the Beast* as reflective of her ambivalent feelings regarding sexuality. Like other maidens in other tales, she shies away from physical intimacy. In many children's stories, prospective suitors are characterized as wild or ravenous animals that nevertheless possess a certain magnetism. The dilemma is thus sharply drawn: The young ladies await the onset of sexual experience with a mixture of eagerness and grievous trepidation.

Little Red Riding Hood plays on this tension and explores the theme of innocence corrupted. On the way to see her ailing grandmother, the girl meets a seducer in the form of a famished wolf and abandons her route as a precautionary measure. Red Riding Hood knows that she cannot fend off the wolf's advances,

so she directs him to her grandmother's house, assuming the older woman will know how to deal with him. When the girl eventually arrives at the cottage, the disguised wolf fascinates her. Unsure of his identity, she agrees to disrobe and join him in bed, asking with wonder about "grandmother's" big arms, ears, eyes, and teeth. But she unwittingly pushes the limits of childish sexuality too far, and the wolf devours her.

In Beauty's tale the outcome is more romantic. The maiden forms her first love relationship with her father, and the sweetness of this familial bond makes sex seem vile to her. Fated to live with the Beast, however, she is forced to question her girlish assumptions. The Beast detains her unfairly but treats her well. She slowly grows fond of him, although she refuses to marry, put off by his ugliness. When she makes a brief visit to her father, she dreams that the Beast is dying because he misses her so terribly. Rushing back to his side, Beauty finds that her nightmare is true. She begs the Beast not to die, crying that she cannot live without him. This blossoming of love makes an adult relationship possible—even beautiful—as the Beast transforms into a handsome prince.

CHAPTER 2

The Battle of the Sexes

ccording to Plato's classical dialogue the *Symposium,* written during the fourth century BC, when the gods created the human race, "human nature was not like the present, but different. The sexes were not two as they are now, but originally three in number; there was man, woman, and the union of the two." Each human being, moreover, was round like a ball, had four hands and four feet, and had "one head with two faces, looking opposite ways, set on a round neck."

Like other creatures of Greek myth, Plato went on to say, the four-legged humans were not content with their lot, and in time they made the mistake of challenging the gods on Mount Olympus. Rather than killing the would-be invaders, Zeus, king of the gods, decided he would merely diminish their power. Accompanied by his son Apollo, Zeus "cut men in two, like a sorb apple which is halved for pickling . . . and he bade Apollo give the face and the half of the neck a turn in order that the man might contemplate the section of himself."

Then Plato brought the story up to date. "Each of us," he wrote, "is but the indenture of a man, and he is always looking for his other half." Men formed from halves of the original males search for others of their kind, he explained, to re-create their wholly masculine ancestors; similarly, women created from the first females seek lovers of the same sex. Those descended from the third gender—the androgyne—seek a mate of the opposite sex. "This meeting and melting into one another, this becoming one instead of two," is, according to the *Symposium,* "the very expression of an ancient need. . . . Human nature was originally one and we were a whole, and the desire and pursuit of the whole is called love."

As an urban sophisticate living at the height of classical Greek culture, Plato may well have meant his story allegorically rather than as literal truth. Yet the theme he evoked was a recurrent one throughout the ancient world. One of the Bible's two accounts of the origins of Adam and Eve, for instance, records that God created humankind as "male and female," a phrase that has traditionally been interpreted by some Jewish and Christian commentators to mean that Adam was originally hermaphroditic—a man on his right side and a woman on his left. God, it is supposed, then separated the two with an axe. Similarly, the Hindu Upanishad traditions have it that Atman, or Being, was lonely until "he divided into two parts, from whence came Man and Woman."

Such tales address one of the most pervasive dualities in human thought: the inescapable division of masculinity and femininity. Based on the obvious physical differences between men and women, the matter of gender also encompasses the cultural expectations about how men and women ought to behave. In mystical and religious traditions throughout the world, gender is often bound up with a host of other dualities: The Chinese yin and yang principles, for example, are associated not only with femininity and masculinity but with shadow and light, warmth and cold, and even moisture and dryness.

Nor have scientific researchers neglected the fascinating puzzle of gender. Over the past two centuries, experimenters in various fields have sought to determine how and if a person's anatomical sex dictates gender behavior in areas as diverse as verbal and visual skills, intuition, and aggression. To date, however, the inconclusive results of their research have generated more heat than light.

Other gender associations, of course, have been less innocuous. Historically, many cultures that classify phenomena in terms of opposites have perceived women as emotional, passive, and even evil while seeing men as rational, active, and virtuous. (The word *virtue* itself comes from the Latin *virtut,* or "masculine.") For those who hold such beliefs, it has often seemed in everyone's best interest for women to be "kept in their place" or protected by their moral and intellectual superiors—men.

Yet as Plato's fable illustrates, even a society as sexually polarized as ancient Greece, in which women were all but excluded from public life or legal protection, perceived a need to bring the two genders together—not only for procreation but for love and companionship. And in every age, mystic seekers have pondered their own inner duality of gender as they seek to reconcile the masculine and feminine traits within themselves.

Gender was in all likelihood a far simpler matter in the earliest human societies. In such cultures, according to many anthropologists, the most significant difference between the sexes was the female capacity to bear children. Because early human beings probably did not associate sexual intercourse with pregnancy and childbirth, women were logically seen as the sole life-givers. In time, that connection may well have extended to a kind of mystical feminine influence over animal and plant fertility as well.

On the practical level, pregnancies and the demands of infant care probably encouraged early women to specialize in tasks close to home such as gathering plants; men took on the more extended trips required to hunt animals. Certainly, by the dawn of recorded history, women and female deities were already associated with agriculture, the harvest, the seasons, and life itself. The vision of the fertile earth as universal mother is among the oldest of mythical conceptions.

Men, it is thought, took on a complementary role. The tasks of the hunter, and later the warrior, required what came to be considered masculine virtues: physical bravery, tactical ingenuity, aggression. On a symbolic level, men were increasingly identified with the beasts they hunted. From carvings found in rock shelters of the twenty-fifth millennium BC to the bulls worshiped in the labyrinth of Minoan Crete, horns and horned beasts stood for the masculine principle just as fecund goddesses represented the feminine.

Conventional wisdom once assumed that this likely division of prehistoric labor evolved smoothly into the familiar male-dominated societies of the classical world. In the late nineteenth century, however, some researchers suggested quite a different scenario. According to their view, most prehistoric cultures deified a supreme goddess and revered women in everyday life as well. That theory aroused little interest until the 1970s and 1980s, when a new generation of goddess researchers, many of them archaeologists or paleoanthropologists, began amassing what they saw as supporting evidence for early goddess worship. As their findings reached print, more and more scholars came to agree with art historian Merlin Stone that "at the very dawn of religion, God was a woman."

As Stone and others reconstruct the story, goddess worship began during the Paleolithic period, or Old Stone Age, an era that lasted from about 2,000,000 BC to approximately 10,000 BC. Although there is some suggestion of this in ancient lore and the customs of modern-day tribal peoples, the case for Paleolithic goddess worship rests mainly on the scores of female statuettes carved by Ice Age peoples in Europe and Asia from such diverse materials as coal, limestone, and the ivory tusks and teeth of the great woolly mammoth. Paleolithic cave

paintings of abstract female images offer additional support for the goddess theory.

Typically, these artifacts—some of them created as early as 30,000 BC—show a life-giving deity with exaggerated breasts and vulva, who is frequently depicted bearing or giving birth to a child. Some still show traces of red ocher, thought to symbolize life-sustaining blood. Often the goddess is accompanied by images of a powerful horned and hoofed animal, such as a bull or a bison, which various scholars believe was meant to suggest a complementary interaction between the male and female principles in nature.

Other researchers, however, remain uncertain whether goddess worship even existed during this period. Without written records, they point out, the meaning of artifacts can be highly elusive. From the point of view of many researchers, anthropologist Ruth Gruhn of McGill University has commented, theories about prehistoric goddess cultures are "on thin ice." What goddess researchers have, she says, is only "a plausible interpretation."

Worship of a female deity is better documented during the Neolithic period, or New Stone Age, which began in about 10,000 BC and which encompassed the development of writing and the beginning of recorded history. By the Neolithic age, records suggest, the goddess answered to different names in different cultures. In Egypt, she was called Nut, the deity who swallowed the sun every evening and gave birth to dawn the following morning. In Sumeria, the goddess had several names; as Nammu, she gave birth to both heaven and earth. And in China, she was called Nü Kwa, "she who established the patterns of existence." Myths about the goddess often incorporated a junior male god, sometimes depicted as her son and lover, who—like the crops in the field—died annually in winter only to be reborn in spring.

As represented by their archaeo-

The primal concept of the Mother Goddess—herself the substance as well as the originator of creation— is captured in this anonymous seventeenth-century engraving. The goddess and her attendant beasts all give nourishment to her human children.

Flanked by other images of the Great Mother, modern-day goddess worshiper Donna Wilshire cradles a statue of the Mayan version of the deity, Ixchel. Trained as an actress, Wilshire sees her carefully researched performances of goddess myths as "sacred work," in which "I can use my whole self."

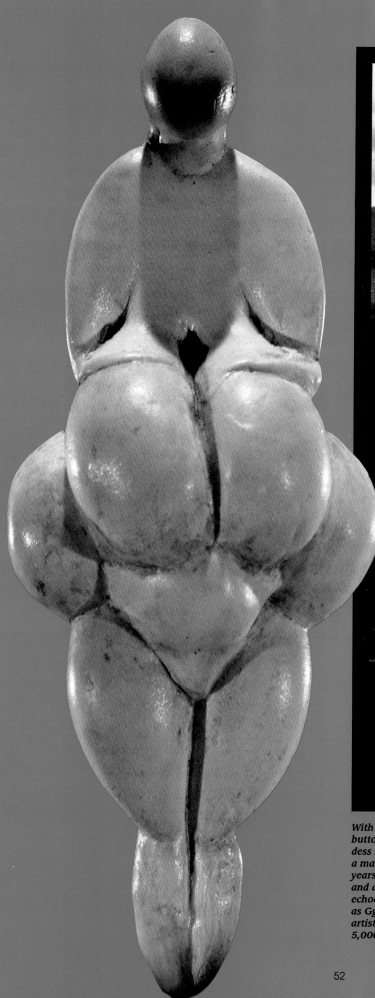

With generous breasts and buttocks, the pocket-size goddess image at left—carved from a mammoth's tusk 25,000 years ago—embodies fertility and abundance. Its shape was echoed in massive temples such as Ggantija, seen above in an artist's conception. Built some 5,000 years ago on the Maltese island of Gozo, the temple's inner chambers outlined the bodies of two females; the doorways symbolized the entrances to their wombs. Worshipers sometimes slept and then awoke within the walls, say researchers, to ritually reenact death and rebirth from the body of the Mother Goddess.

logical remains, the goddess-worshiping societies of the Neolithic era were remarkably peaceful and egalitarian. Strikingly absent from the artifacts of these cultures are fortified walls, heavy weaponry, or great economic disparity—which would be indicated, for instance, by extreme variations in living space among different classes. Even ritual sacrifice was probably unknown. Reporting on his excavations in modern Turkey of the seventh-millennium city of Catal Hüyük, archaeologist James Mellaart wrote, "There was an ordered pattern of society. There were no human or animal sacrifices. Vegetarianism prevailed, for domestic animals were kept for milk and wool—not for meat. Above all, the supreme deity in all the temples was a goddess."

According to modern students of the goddess, the Neolithic goddess cultures were women-centered in daily life as well. Judging by the pictorial record of Minoan Crete, for example, the women there played a leading role in all aspects of daily life, serving as priestesses and as the heads of family clans. They took part in financial and business matters, owned homes and other property, and even functioned as judges and magistrates. Children, as they probably did in the Paleolithic age, inherited family names and property matrilineally, through their mothers.

Although women held positions of prestige in goddess cultures, goddess researchers contend that there was a rough equality between the sexes; neither outranked the other. For example, even though the Cretans almost certainly worshiped a single goddess, their religious rituals venerated bulls and other horned beasts clearly linked to the masculine principle. Cretan friezes and other artifacts show girls and boys participating equally in ritual bull-leaping dances and men serving as priests beside the more numerous priestesses.

One magnificent remnant of the Neolithic goddess worshipers is a great sacred edifice on the small island of Gozo, about four miles from Malta in the Mediterranean Sea. Known locally as Ggantija, or "the Giant," the ruin consists of two temples, built of gray stone blocks weighing as much as forty to fifty tons, that share a common wall. One of the structures, with an interior axis 100 feet long, is commonly identified as the mother of the pair; the other, somewhat smaller in size, as the daughter. Inside each temple, oval chambers, accessible only through narrow entrance halls thought to represent the birth canal, reflect the rounded forms of the many female icons that have been unearthed near the site.

Little is known about the culture that built Ggantija, although archaeologists believe the structure was probably erected sometime between 3600 and 3000 BC by a people who used only stone and horn tools. According to local tradition, however, the temples were built single-handedly by a female ruler nursing a baby. After a strengthening meal of magic beans, islanders say, the woman transported the enormous stones to the temple site in one day. That night, she constructed the immense double walls that surround the temples. Researchers suggest that the legendary woman is a memory of the goddess herself, for whom Ggantija was presumably built.

By the time that the temple reached its completion, though, the goddess-centered societies of central Europe and the Middle East had already begun to disappear. With the dawning of the Iron Age and the development of effective swords, spears, and other weaponry, warlike nomadic peoples from Europe and Asia launched a series of ruthless invasions from the

A powerful phallus distinguishes this bronze figure of Frey, the Norse fertility god. Such images symbolized the male-centered order that supplanted the Mother Goddess.

north, recorded archaeologically in burned and looted cities throughout the Mediterranean region.

Just as the goddess cultures had linked farming and the harvest cycle to the feminine principle, so the newcomers had evolved a connection between hunting and fighting—the chief activities of their cultures—and the masculine. At first, the northerners' gods were simply personified as male warriors, associated with lightning, thunder, and the sky. In time, these figures became kings and lawgivers who ruled from the heavens rather than from the earth.

Around the world a new kind of masculine hero developed, one whom mythologist Joseph Campbell has dubbed "the hero with a thousand faces." According to Campbell, this mythical figure, who embodies masculine ideals of courage, cunning, and strength, typically passes through hardship, gains a great good through personal suffering, and brings the reward to humankind. Along the way, he sometimes encounters the feminine principle, either in the guise of the old, benevolent goddess or as a sensual temptress such as a mermaid or a beautiful but evil witch.

ther myths recorded the great social transformation from feminine to masculine deities. One of the earliest is the Sumerian tale of the slaying of Tiamat, mother of the gods. According to the Sumerians, Tiamat, a goddess associated with the sea, gave birth to a succession of marvelous creatures who included—to her ultimate undoing—a group of male sky gods. When the young gods heard Tiamat's consort urging her to destroy them because of the noise they made, they decided to kill her first. Seeing an opportunity for supreme kingship over his brothers, the god Marduk volunteered for the traitorous task.

Arming himself with a bow, arrows, a mace, and a large net, Marduk rode toward his mother in a swirling thunderstorm. A great battle ensued, until at last Marduk managed to wrap the goddess in his net and force a blast of wind into her open mouth, rendering her temporarily helpless. Taking advantage of Tiamat's weakness, he shot an arrow into her heart and killed her.

Although Tiamat had already created the cosmos long before, Marduk now fashioned it anew from pieces of her carcass. With one half of her body he made the sky, with the other half, the earth. And from Tiamat's sightless eyes poured two great rivers, the Tigris and the Euphrates, the cradle of Sumerian civilization.

With the death of the Mother Goddess and the cultures that had worshiped her, a patriarchal social order emerged, one in which men dominated not only women but one another as well. Even the emblems of authority changed as the new order consolidated its hold on Middle Eastern society. By the fifth century BC, according to classical scholar Eva Keuls in her 1985 book *Reign of the Phallus,* the phallus itself had become the standard symbol of power—political, social, and moral—in much of the classical world. In monumental obelisks and columns, hand-carried swords and spears, and heavily ornamented codpieces, the link between power and the phallic symbol of masculinity would endure for centuries.

While men of the new male-dominated era began the series of triumphs and tragedies that led to modern civilization, women's status deteriorated around the world. Considered the property of their fathers, husbands, or brothers, women had little or no say in economic, political, or even religious matters.

The Greek philosopher Aristotle—who charged that women have a fundamental moral weakness—went so far as to deny women any part in the creation of life, insisting that women played no genetic role in reproduction. In India it was said that Hindu women must be reborn as men before they could achieve enlightenment. And in China, the sage Confucius taught that women should be subservient to their spiritually superior husbands. The devaluation of women is evident in a popular Chinese poem of the third century: "How sad it is to be a woman, / Nothing on earth is held so cheap. / Boys stand leaning at the door / Like Gods fallen out of heaven. / Their hearts brave the Four Oceans. / The wind and dust of a thousand miles. / No one is glad when a girl is born: / By her the family sets no store." So pervasive were such attitudes that when, in the late twentieth century, the Chinese government attempted to limit families to only one child, the number of murdered female infants rose alarmingly in some rural areas. By killing a daughter, the families could try again for a son.

In many lands, temples once dedicated to a goddess were converted into holy sites for the new male-oriented religions.

The Parthenon of the Acropolis in Athens, for example, had been a shrine of the goddess Athena since 1300 BC. In AD 450 it was converted into a Christian church.

Even the old symbols of the earth goddess were suppressed or transformed into tokens of evil. In the biblical story of Adam and Eve, the snake, a one-time symbol of regeneration and wisdom, became a traitor that seduced Eve into sampling forbidden fruit. Similarly, eating the sacred fruit, an act reminiscent of the rites of Egyptian goddess worshipers, brought only the knowledge of evil and expulsion from Eden.

Because of its importance to Judaism, Christianity, and Islam, the story of Adam and Eve is considered by many scholars to be a turning point in the Western view of the role of men and women in society. "I shall call you Eve [Hebrew for 'life'] because you are the mother of all living things," Adam announces when Eve is first created. But while her name recalls the fecundity of the Mother Goddess, Eve herself is created from Adam's rib and thus placed in a secondary, subservient position to him, becoming what one commentator has ruefully called a kind of "permanent second mate." In his letter to the Corinthians, Christ's disciple Paul used the story of Adam and Eve to argue that women must veil their heads in church to show their subordination to men. "For man was not made from woman, but woman from man," he wrote. "Neither was man created for woman, but woman for man."

Eve's subsequent disobedience, which brought about the downfall and misery of all humanity, was a sign to later male commentators that women were morally inferior to men. Although heroines and positive examples of womanhood can be found throughout the Old and New Testaments, it was

This fourteenth-century Italian fresco depicts God creating Eve from Adam's rib—a story taken as proof of male superiority. As goddess worship declined, so too did the status of women.

Titled simply Sin, this 1893 painting by German artist Franz Stuck presents an updated portrayal of Eve, the first woman in the biblical creation story. Seductive and apparently ready for new wickedness, she seems quite at home with the serpent that coils about her shoulders. For centuries, in images like this one, women carried the blame for humankind's loss of innocence.

The Mystery of the Black Madonna

Peppered across Europe in shrines, crypts, and cathedrals are hundreds of enigmatic images of a dark-skinned woman, worshiped today as the Black Madonna. Whether carved of ebony, stone, or gray cedar or painted in brilliant colors, the dark woman appears in splendor—against a golden background, ornately garbed, adorned with gems, and crowned. She holds a child and is sometimes attended by the moon and stars. Her adherents call her "the queen of heaven" and look to her for fertility and miraculous healings.

Perhaps the most famous black madonna, Our Lady of Czestochowa *(below, right)* has been venerated as the "queen of Poland" since 1656. More recently, Pope John Paul II embraced her as his personal icon, and members of the banned Solidarity labor movement wore her image as an underground badge. But her worship dates from the early Christian church.

As the Church received converts from the "heathenism" of goddess worship, it offered them the Virgin Mary as a devotional figure. Many pre-Christian Mother Goddess images were simply renamed. In this way, icons crafted with black faces to suggest the Great Mother's richest soil, the dark of the moon, and death became black madonnas. Other black-skinned images that became known as madonnas reached Europe from the Middle East in the baggage of traders, Roman soldiers, and returning Phoenician sailors.

Unnerved perhaps by the fervor of her adherents, Church officials sometimes suggested the darkness of the Black Madonna's many faces was accidental—brought on by age or candle smoke. But this explanation seems unlikely; ebony was obviously chosen for some of the images, and no amount of smoke could darken the Virgin Mary's sunny nature to match the Black Madonna's complex, earth mother attributes.

Eve who became the symbol for all women, who were blamed for every wickedness in the world because of her great lapse. A typical commentary came in the second century from the Christian theologian Tertullian. "Do you not know that each of you is also an Eve?" he wrote. "You are the devil's gateway, you are the unsealer of that forbidden tree, you are the first deserter of that divine law, you are the one who persuaded him whom the devil was too weak to attack. How easily you destroyed man, the image of God! Because of the death which you brought upon us, even the son of God had to die." Or as the prophet Muhammad put it more succinctly in the seventh century, "When Eve was created, Satan rejoiced."

For his part, Adam (from the Hebrew *adham,* meaning "man") makes an almost equally poor showing in the creation story, appearing at best a gullible dupe. His defects as a male role model were soon remedied, however, by the great patriarchs of the Old Testament—Abraham, Isaac, and Jacob—who set the accepted Judeo-Christian standard for masculine leadership and strength.

During the Dark Ages in Europe, philosophy and other forms of book learning were preserved for the most part by Christian monastic orders, whose celibate male members saw women primarily as sexual temptresses in conscious or unconscious league with Satan. By the sixth century, the writings of misogynistic theologians led to a controversy within the Church as to whether women had souls at all. To resolve the matter, fifty-nine bishops assembled in 585 at Mâcon in eastern France. After some learned debate, the bishops cast their ballots: Women were determined to have souls—but by a majority of only one vote.

Not every branch of Christianity, however, saw Eve's role in such pejorative terms. The Gnostic Christians—an early sect who believed that God could be experienced directly through personal

spiritual insight, or *gnosis*—looked upon the Genesis story as an allegory of spiritual self-discovery. According to their view, Adam represents the human psyche and Eve the higher principle, the spiritual self. By encouraging Adam to eat of the forbidden fruit, Eve awakens Adam to an awareness of his spiritual nature. In the Gnostic text *Reality of the Rulers,* Adam speaks of Eve in terms reminiscent of goddess worship: "It is you who have given me life: you shall be called Mother of the Living; for it is she who is my Mother. It is she who is the Physician, and the Woman, and She Who Has Given Birth."

Traces of goddess worship lingered in mainstream culture as well, often in the form of lesser female deities subordinate to the new male gods. In many European peasant communities, rituals once associated with the goddess were transferred wholesale to the Virgin Mary *(page 58).* So close was the connection for some between the old fertility goddesses and the Virgin of the new order that beliefs grew up associating Mary with fertile harvests. It was said that when Mary traveled with Joseph and the Holy Infant through Egypt, nearby wheat fields sprang into full growth as she passed by.

Ordinary women also retained a certain mystical power, especially those old enough to have passed the dangerous years of childbirth. In Europe, older women often served as midwives, healers, or, more sinisterly, as witches, capable of brewing love potions, poisons, and herbal cures. In the fifteenth, sixteenth, and seventeenth centuries, however, this remaining bastion of feminine power was crushed by frenzied witch hunts that resulted in the deaths of an estimated 200,000 accused witches throughout Europe. The vast majority of these victims were women, for it was believed that women were more susceptible to obeying the

As the hangman checks the corpses of four women executed as witches, a witch finder (at right in this seventeenth-century English engraving) collects a fee for accusing them. Medieval witch hunters declared women weaker and more sensuous than men, thus far easier for the devil to woo into witchcraft.

voice of the devil. "All witchcraft comes from carnal lust, which in women is insatiable," pronounced the *Malleus Maleficarum,* the fifteenth-century text that helped promote and justify the witch prosecutions. "Wherefore for the sake of fulfilling their lusts they consort even with devils."

With the modern Industrial Revolution, however, many aspects of society—including the status of women—began to change slowly. By the twentieth century, reformed divorce and property laws, more effective birth control, and safer obstetrical practices had fundamentally altered the facts of female life. Among the minor side effects of this vast transformation was a resurgence of goddess worship among women repelled by the masculine orientation of conventional faiths. By the end of the 1980s, an estimated 100,000 women in the United States alone actively worshiped the goddess in rites that ranged from baking edible versions of the Paleolithic earth mother to celebrating the mysteries of human blood and milk.

Meanwhile, a small number of men began developing "male mythopoetic groups" as a kind of masculine counterpart to goddess worship. According to the *Wall Street Journal,* which described male rites that included beating on drums, wrestling in mud, weeping openly, and urinating to-

Australian Aborigines in 1988 reenact in ritual dance a creation myth many thousands of years old. Explained one tribesman, "Earth our mother, eagle our cousin. Tree, he is pumping our blood. And we are all one."

gether on trees, participants in the male and female worship groups often see their work as complementary. When a group of men found their mythopoetic rituals interrupted by the primal screams of goddess worshipers farther down the same Los Angeles hill, some were annoyed, the *Journal* reported. But others considered the moment a magical one. "There was a sense of communication, of being whole with the women, even if it just happened on a psychic level," said one man. "It was the epitome of sacredness in the 1990s."

For her part, meanwhile, the much deprecated Eve still casts a considerable mythical shadow over the most technological of twentieth-century studies. In 1986, researchers exploring the so-called genetic history of the human race discovered evidence of a true original mother. By examining individual variations in mitochondrial DNA, a type of cell material passed on from mother to child, the researchers traced the descent and prehistoric movements of various populations. Much to their surprise, the computer analysis also suggested that all humans share at least one common female ancestor, an African woman of about 200,000 years ago whose descendants in every generation have included at least one female to pass on her mitochondrial signature. Without need for explanation, the geneticists named the woman Eve.

As that discovery suggests, questions about masculine and feminine nature once reserved for the philosopher have increasingly become the province of scientists, from genetic researchers to physicians, anthropologists, neurologists,

and even students of parapsychology. At the heart of the gender research undertaken by these and other scholars is a single issue: whether biology or society—or both—determines male and female behavior traits.

Among the first scientists to consider the roots of gender identity was Sigmund Freud, the Viennese psychiatrist who in the late nineteenth and early twentieth centuries developed the science of psychoanalysis, the so-called talking cure for mental illness. Freud, whose daughter Anna became a prominent psychoanalyst in her own right, once wrote that "Anatomy is destiny." By that, he did not mean that gender behavior—whether to wear a dress or trousers, for instance—was genetically programmed, but that possessing the anatomical equipment of a given sex influenced the mental development of any child so profoundly as to determine much of the youngster's future personality.

Thus, according to Freud, little boys developed the "castration complex," a subconscious fear of losing their penises, while little girls fell prey to "penis envy." Small boys were attracted sexually to their mothers, the "first women" in their lives, and were jealous of their fathers—a family scenario Freud dubbed the Oedipus complex, after the classical Greek hero who killed his father and married his mother. Similarly, little girls flirted with their fathers while assuming a cooler attitude to-

Urban American men go tribal with a backrub chain (above) during a weekend Wildman Gathering in a Texas forest. In search of a deeper understanding of masculinity, some 50,000 men flocked to all-male retreats like this one during the 1980s. Many of the seekers were inspired by poet Robert Bly (inset), who urged modern men to try to get in touch with the "large, primitive man" within.

ward their mothers. Those who failed to surmount these early crises, said Freud, could be mired in self-destructive neuroses in later life, but those who resolved their conflicts successfully would grow into normally adjusted men and women, with the appropriate behaviors of their gender.

In the century that followed, some critics found many of the details of Freud's theories far more applicable to men than to women. Harking back to the Paleolithic power of the Mother Goddess, they argued that for every woman who experiences penis envy there is a man enduring womb envy because of his inability to bear and deliver children. Classical examples of this secret wish include stories that describe Zeus giving birth to the goddess Athena (from his head) and the wine god Dionysius (from a cavity in his leg).

Such revisionism notwithstanding, the door Freud had opened into an area of hitherto unmentionable topics remained ajar, ready for other researchers to enter.

A very different scholarly exploration of gender began in the autumn of 1931, when a young anthropologist named Margaret Mead sailed with her new husband, Reo Fortune—also an anthropologist—for New Guinea, a Pacific island with a vast assortment of diverse cultures and religions. The two hoped to study a highly ceremonial people who lived on a grassy plain beyond the Torricelli Mountains, the island's northern coastal range. But the mountain journey, difficult under the best circumstances, proved impossible after Mead injured her ankle and had to be carried along the slippery trail.

Halfway to the northern plains, the young couple found themselves stranded in a mountain village "with no one to move our six months' supplies in either direction—into the interior or back to the coast," Mead later recalled. They had no choice "but to settle down, build a house, and work with the simple, impoverished Mountain Arapesh, who had little ritual and less art, among whom we now found ourselves."

For Margaret Mead, the frustrating delay turned out to be a blessing in disguise. From her and her husband's work with the Arapesh and later with the Mundugumor and the Tchambuli, two other tribes of New Guinea, Mead developed a new perspective on gender identity that served as the primary focus of her 1935 classic, *Sex and Temperament.* In that book Mead argued that the role or temperament of each gender, including the dominance of one over the other, is cultural rather than biological in origin.

"Neither the Arapesh nor the Mundugumor profit by a contrast between the sexes," she wrote. "The Arapesh ideal is the mild, responsive man married to the mild, responsive woman; the Mundugumor ideal is the violent aggressive man married to the violent aggressive woman. In the third tribe, the Tchambuli, we found a genuine reversal of the sex-attitudes of our own culture, with the woman the dominant, impersonal, managing partner, the man the less responsible and the emotionally dependent person." Contrasting traditional Western expectations with the personality traits assigned to each gender by the New Guinean cultures, Mead concluded that "we no longer have any basis for regarding such aspects of behavior as sex-linked."

Mead's was by no means the last word, however. By the 1950s, yet another specialty, the controversial discipline of sociobiology, had joined the nature-versus-nurture battle over gender identity. Proponents of this approach disagreed wholeheartedly with Mead, arguing instead that our genes preprogram human behavior, including the feminine and masculine roles. According to their theory of coevolution, men and women who choose behaviors that tend to promote their families' survival—in a pet example, couples who assign childcare to the woman and survival tasks to the presumably stronger man—are more likely to pass on their genes, and with their genes, their life choices.

Other scientists, who include the well-known paleontologist Stephen Jay Gould, strongly disagree with the sociobiologists, arguing that fossils show little change in human brain structure or size in 50,000 years and that over that comparatively short period of time only cultural evolution—that is, social adaptation—is possible. According to these researchers, children learn their gender, and the behaviors associated with it, only as they grow up in a given society.

One condition often thought to shed light on the question of gender identity is hermaphroditism, the development in a single human being of both male and female sexual organs. Cases of hermaphroditism have been reported through the ages, often with fanciful explanations. The term itself com-

Male and female merge in this statue of Hermaphroditos, the revered Greek god who was born male, but whose body was later joined with that of a nymph who loved him. Deities symbolizing the unity of both genders also appeared in the traditions of India, Egypt, and Central and North America.

Bold Amazon horsewomen are victorious in battle on this silver-and-gold chariot panel, crafted in the Greek city-state of Ionia in the sixth century BC. The legendary women warriors were said to claim for themselves all the exploits and independence that other societies reserved for men.

memorates Hermaphroditos, the son of Hermes and Aphrodite, who, according to Greek myth, was said to have joined in one body with the nymph Salmacis while bathing in a lake. During the second century a more plausible, though equally erroneous, theory was proposed by the Greek physician Galen, who argued that male babies were created with semen from the right testicle, female babies with semen from the left, and hermaphrodite babies with a mixture of semen from both testicles.

Modern medical research explains the matter more prosaically: Human hermaphrodites, it seems, owe their condition to a rare error in the reproductive process. Ordinarily, a child's sex is determined at conception, when the female egg, which contains an X sex chromosome, joins with the male sperm, which may carry either an X or a Y sex chromosome. If the resulting combination is XX, the baby will be a girl; if it is XY, the baby will be a boy. Hermaphroditism occurs in those rare cases when the message sent by the chromosome pair becomes garbled, leading the embryo to develop both male and female sex characteristics.

Despite their bodies' ambiguous status, people born with hermaphroditism almost always see themselves as being of only one gender, either male or female. Experts now advise parents of a hermaphrodite to decide whether they have a son or daughter—and stick to that decision—before their child reaches the age of eighteen months. Afterward, they say, the child's gender identity locks in and is difficult, if not impossible, to reverse.

While hermaphrodites challenge accepted notions of sex and gender, the more common, though still unusual, case of transsexuals—physiological men or women who nevertheless identify themselves with the opposite sex—is in some respects still more baffling. No genetic, hormonal, or environmental factor has been found to explain the transsexual's psychological urge. Yet once the transsexual impulse is established—usually in early childhood—no amount of psychological counseling will reverse it.

"I was born with the wrong body, being feminine by gender but male by sex," explained one transsexual, "and I could achieve completeness only when the one was adjusted to the other." Like many other modern-day transsexuals, this man later underwent rigorous hormone therapy and sex-change surgery to make his external sexual appearance match his internal feelings of gender.

The history of transsexualism, like that of hermaphroditism, is an ancient one. As early as the fourth century BC, Hippocrates wrote of the Scythian "No-men" who "show feminine inclinations and behave as women." Almost 500 years later, the Jewish philosopher Philo Judaeus commented on the desperate actions taken by some Alexandrian men who wished to be women: "Expending every possible care on their outward adornment, they are not ashamed even to employ every device to change artificially their nature as men into women—some of them craving a complete transformation into women, they have amputated their generative members."

Female transsexualism was a recurrent theme in classical Greek accounts of the Amazons, a supposed race of warrior women from Asia Minor who were said to be descended directly from Ares, the god of war. Described by some feminist historians as a distorted memory of the old woman-centered cultures, theirs was a matriarchal society in which women governed and fought and men took care of household tasks. One tradition had it that the women were so fierce that they burned or cut off their right breasts to make it easier to shoot a bow and arrow. It is from this practice that they received the name Amazon, "without breast." Greek artists apparently did not take the story too literally, however, because Greek vases and sculptures invariably depict Amazon warriors with unmutilated bosoms.

As Greek knowledge of the surrounding territory grew, the country of the Amazons shifted position so that it was always just beyond the boundaries of the known world. Among many reported contacts with the tribe was an account concerning the Amazon queen Thalestris, said to have visited Alexander the Great during one of his Asian campaigns in hopes of conceiving a daughter by him.

Amazons remained a subject of half-believed European travelers' tales well into the sixteenth century. During one of his trips to South America, the Elizabethan explorer Sir Walter Raleigh heard secondhand accounts of Amazons. "They meet with men but once in a year," he later wrote. "At that time all the Kings of the borders assemble, and the Queens of the Amazons, and after the Queens have chosen, the rest cast lots for their Valentines. This one month they feast, dance and drink of their wines in abundance, and the Moon being done, they all depart to their own Provinces."

Other European explorers encountered a similar phenomenon among the Tupinamba of Brazil. In this culture, according to a contemporary report by the explorer Pedro de Magalhães de Gandavo, certain women "follow men's pursuits as if they were not women. They wear the hair cut in the same way as men, and go to war with bows and arrows and pursue game, always in company with men." De Gandavo and others were so struck by this phenomenon that they named Brazil's chief river the Amazon to commemorate the tribe.

Back in Europe, reports of transsexualism included a persistent apocryphal story of a woman pope said to have reigned in the ninth century. According to this legend, "Pope Joan" was a gifted scholar who disguised herself as a man and was chosen by the College of Cardinals to become pope. The new pontiff reigned for two years, five months, and four days, only to die in the year 858 during a church procession as she gave birth to an illegitimate child. Although the story was later debunked by a seventeenth-century French Calvinist who showed conclusively that there was no gap in the succession of male popes, fear that a woman could seize the ultimate font of spiritual authority dictated a physical examination for all new popes until the mid-1500s.

Among modern American Indians, male transsexuals often play the role of a "third gender," in the phrase of anthropologist Walter Williams, who in his 1986 book, entitled *The Spirit and the Flesh,* cites parallel customs in the folk cultures of Siberia, Vietnam, and the Pacific. Dubbed *berdaches,* from the French slang for "transvestite," these men dressed as women play a distinctive role in many American Indian cultures. Although practices vary from tribe to tribe, the berdaches are often credited with shamanistic in-

In this fifteenth-century illustration, a baby spilling from the womb of a ninth-century pope reveals the pontiff's true sex. The tale of Pope Joan, though false, shocked believers during the Middle Ages.

sight and powers of healing. Cheyenne war parties, for instance, almost invariably included a berdache healer because of the transsexual reputation for effecting miracle cures. Berdaches in other tribes perform a variety of social functions, from blessing sacred trees to cooking the food for funerals.

From the American Indian point of view, the life of the berdache is as natural as that of an ordinary man or woman. Berdaches, most tribes agree, are simply "born that way," although their preferences may not be apparent until they reach the age of nine or ten. At that point, young boys with feminine tendencies often undergo special public rituals in which the child can choose or reject the social position of berdache.

This berdache, or "man-woman," photographed on the Standing Rock Sioux Reservation in South Dakota, adopted women's ways after dreaming he was female.

genders, from male and female styles of thinking to feminine intuition and male aggression. Often, scientists find that the expected gender differences evaporate under controlled testing. One of the few exceptions, at least in Western cultures, has to do with the ability to perform different types of intellectual tasks. Studies regularly show that women, on average, have greater verbal ability and men, on average, have greater skill at performing visual tasks and perceiving spatial relations, such as those involving maps, mazes, and three-dimensional objects. The discrepancies between the sexes are so small, however, that many researchers consider them negligible.

Even these slight differences have been brought into question by studies of other cultures. An anthropologist named John Berry, for instance, once conducted considerable research into the visual-spatial skills of both the Canadian Eskimos and the Temne people of Sierra Leone. Berry found no sex differences among the Eskimos, who raise both boys and girls with unconditional love and with considerable freedom to do as they please. By contrast, the Temne, who have a highly disciplined society and rear girls much more strictly than boys, exhibited significant differences between the sexes in visual-spatial abilities. Berry concludes from those results that sex differences in visual-spatial skills may be more pronounced in societies where women have tightly restricted social roles.

Some Western tribes, for instance, place the boy in an enclosure with masculine and feminine artifacts and set fire to the surrounding walls. If the boy rescues the tools associated with women's work from the blaze, he is declared transsexual. A less stressful approach is taken by the Mohave of the Colorado Valley, who stage a ceremony in which a hidden singer performs special songs. A boy unwilling to become a berdache will not respond to the tunes, but one who is truly berdache will dance enthusiastically. Afterward, the boy, dressed in a woman's skirt, proclaims his new feminine name to the assembled group.

With the question of gender identification a stubborn and enduring mystery, many researchers have chosen to focus instead on traits traditionally ascribed to one of the two

Research on brain organization in men and women has been similarly inconclusive. In the 1970s, research revealed a general hemispheric division of labor in all human brains between language and visual-spatial skills. The left hemisphere appears to be the main language center, where the ability to read, write, analyze, and process sequential information is housed. The right side is more holistic; it specializes in visual-spatial skills, and it processes emotions and other nonverbal information. Artistic abilities also seem to reside in the brain's right hemisphere.

ssuming that men and women do indeed differ in their inherent verbal and visual abilities, some researchers have conjectured that women are left-brain oriented because they excel at verbal skills and that men are right-brain oriented because they have superior spatial perception. But others draw just the opposite conclusion: Women must be right-brained because they are better at reading nonverbal messages from people, they reason, and men must be left-brained because they are better at mathematics.

Still other scientists—the majority—believe that the idea that each sex has a dominant brain hemisphere is much too simplistic. Instead, differences in the brain structure between men and women, if any, seem likely to involve the way in which information is passed between the hemispheres. One such theory has been developed by Jerre Levy, a professor of psychology at the University of Chicago. Levy's research suggests that men have highly specialized brain hemispheres, whereas women's brain hemispheres are less functionally distinct. As a result, according to Levy, verbal tasks in women are often handled in both hemispheres of the brain, thus interfering with the right side's ability to perform spatial tasks.

Yet Levy also believes that having less specialized brain hemispheres makes it possible for women to communicate in a faster and more informal way than men. ''This may be at the root of what we call female intuition,'' Levy says, ''the ability of women, which men think illogical, to respond to a danger sensed rather than perceived—'My baby's in trouble'—or to produce a complete character analysis, later often proved right, of someone they've met for only ten minutes.''

The idea that women are more intuitive than men is deeply rooted in both Western and Eastern cultures; in the latter, intuition is associated with the feminine yin, and logic is linked to the masculine yang. Certainly, if the term refers to an ability to perceive other people's feelings and nonverbal signals, ''feminine intuition'' could well be the result of cultural, rather than biological, factors. Cast in the role of nurturer, women must learn how to read the facial expressions, body movements, and other nonverbal messages that reveal when someone is ill, frightened, tired, or angry. In most cultures, men are also taught that logical and rational thinking is more masculine, which may make men less aware of their instinctive perceptions of other people's feelings. By contrast, women are encouraged to be emotional and to express their feelings, including their intuitive ones.

To certain observers, however, feminine intuition means more than good people skills. It includes the power, deeply rooted in the woman's identity as mother, to sense telepathically when a child or a mate, perhaps hundreds of miles away, is in

Upon a lotus seat, symbol of rebirth, a Tantric guru and his lover embrace in sexual union in this woodcut from Nepal. Tantrism celebrates sexual intimacy as a path to cosmic oneness.

In Shiva's holiest shrine in Varanasi, India, a temple priest gives the black Shiva linga—prime emblem of the supreme Hindu god— one of five daily ritual washings with water from the sacred Ganges River. The phallic shaft of black stone in its vulva-shaped base symbolizes the reconciliation, in Shiva, of all opposites; in fact, one of the deity's names—Ardhanarishvara— translates as ''half-woman lord.''

danger. Louisa Rhine, who with her husband, Joseph, helped to found the discipline of parapsychology, argued that this type of paranormal intuition is common to both genders—but only one, the female, tends to be comfortable talking about it.

Although "it is true that many more women than men report ESP experiences," she wrote in 1961 in her book *Hidden Channels of the Mind,* "this difference might be the result of such superficial causes as women being more communicative, less inhibited on this topic than men." The difference between men and women is in the frequency of reports, she pointed out, not in their nature. In one case, for instance, Rhine described a man who correctly predicted the appearance of his firstborn child based on a precognitive dream; in another instance, a father seemed to know when his son—thousands of miles away across the Atlantic during World War II—was deathly ill.

In the controlled conditions of the laboratory, Rhine reported, preadolescent boys and girls do equally well at standard tests of psi powers. Once past adolescence, however, the effects of socialization create a paranormal gender gap in which adult women are likely to score better than adult men. "Along with the difference in scoring level," wrote Rhine, "one usually notices a difference in *attitude* toward the test. A young woman will easily, almost gaily, and in a gamelike spirit take the test." A young man, uncertain about the validity of the test, "would be surprised if he 'got anything.' Whatever he gets, he accepts with reservations. It might have been this, it might have been that. He wants to think it over." In thinking his response over, Rhine added, the man's certainty evaporates—and with it, any evidence of his psi powers.

Whereas most psychologists and parapsychologists tend to agree that feminine intuition—however defined—is a culturally acquired trait rather than a biological one, many scientists still consider aggression to be physically linked to masculinity. This thesis—with which some researchers now disagree—has in turn been used to explain, and sometimes to justify, why men are often found to dominate women in the home, in the workplace, and in politics, and to support the idea that men are more ambitious in the business world, better at sports, and more suited to defend their country's honor in battle. The link between masculinity and aggression has also been used to explain why so many more men than women are involved in violent and criminal acts.

Two major biological theories have been offered to explain male aggression. Both involve the hormone testosterone, which is found in all healthy human beings but is known as a male hormone because it occurs in much higher levels in men. Some researchers believe testosterone is a physiological messenger that triggers aggression. Because men have more testosterone than women, they argue, men are innately more prone to a wide range of aggressive actions, from rough-and-tumble play as children to rowdiness, reckless driving, and robbery as adults. In accordance with that line of reasoning, many societies have castrated men who have a history of violent behavior. It was hoped that by removing the testes, where testosterone is produced in males, the source of male aggression would be eliminated as well. The handful of follow-up studies that have examined the impact of castration on

At once a thoughtful young woman and a wise old man, this double-faced statue guards the tomb of France's sixteenth-century King Francis II, in Nantes Cathedral. Crafted during the heyday of alchemy, the figure symbolized for some the ideal of the divine androgyne—a self equally male and female.

Annie Lennox, lead singer of the Eurhythmics rock duo, flouts conventional standards of beauty with an aloof androgyny. Many popular performers, spurning—or merging—notions of rugged male and yielding female, achieve an ambiguous presence intended to intrigue both sexes. While some experts attribute this allure to the power of the hidden and the forbidden in human sexuality, others see in it a healthy recognition of the opposite-sex traits each person carries within.

aggression and violence, however, seem to rule out the simple testosterone theory. In a 1959 study in Norway, for example, nine of sixteen castrated men eventually died as a result of aggressive encounters—hardly an indication of newly peaceable natures. Studies involving rhesus monkeys have also failed to show any relationship between castration and a lessening of aggressive behavior.

In light of such evidence, some scientists have propounded a different biological explanation of male aggression, one that focuses on prenatal exposure to the testosterone produced by the Y sex chromosome early in the development of a male embryo. These scientists believe that this early exposure to the hormone affects brain formation in such a way as to predispose boys to greater physical activity and to learning aggression. Yet studies of girls who were exposed to unusual levels of prenatal testosterone (often as a result of hormone supplements taken by their mothers during pregnancy) have failed to produce strong confirmation of this theory. As with the study of feminine intuition, the question of male aggression remains open.

While science ponders the puzzling social and biological brew that makes up each gender's identity, the sexual duality itself continues to challenge students of the human condition. In every age and country, mystics have sought to unify these opposites, to join the divided halves of humanity into one whole.

In the East, this urge toward sexual reunification—and thus human perfection—is expressed most strongly in the Tantric traditions of Hinduism and Buddhism. According to the Tantras, a series of highly esoteric texts that become fully explicable only with the aid of a spiritual master, enlightenment is a matter of reuniting the masculine principle Shiva, said to reside in the crown of one's head, with the feminine Shakti, found at the base of the spine. By awakening Shakti, adepts hope to encourage her to rise upward toward Shiva through a succession of bodily power centers called chakras.

One of many Tantric techniques for aiding Shakti's upward progress is *chakra-puja,* or "circle worship," in which an equal number of male and female adepts gather together in a circle for a ceremonial meal of wine, meat, fish, and bread. After dinner, the participants pair off for ritual sex, in which the man represents Shiva, the woman, Shakti. In so-called right-handed Tantra, in which each woman sits to the right of her male partner, the sexual act is privately visualized rather than actually consummated. But in the left-handed school, in which women sit to the left, physical union is considered necessary.

Because Tantric adepts seek to isolate their sexual energies from lust or even love, devotees often deliberately seek out ugly partners. Still other groups steer clear of emotional entanglements by assigning partners randomly. One custom, for example, calls for each woman to drop her bodice in a common pile. Each man then picks a bodice and is assigned the corresponding partner.

In the mating that follows, both man and woman are said to gain a form of sexual energy that itself helps lead them to inner enlightenment. "The man who knows the fiery form of Shiva procreates himself anew at every intercourse," records one of the Tantras. "His body glows, his mind is crystal clear, his spirit is in harmony with heaven."

Sexual magic—if only on the symbolic level—has also had its influence on the Western alchemical tradition. Although medieval European alchemists often worked in husband-and-wife teams, most placed a greater emphasis on achieving a balanced awareness of the male and female traits within themselves, to become, at least in a spiritual sense, the perfect union of the two.

Thus, the twentieth-century French alchemist Eugene Canseliet was pleased, but not surprised, by an unusual meeting he had with the elusive mystic Fulcanelli, a shadowy figure who was himself a French alchemist, in 1954. In that year, Canseliet later said, he found himself mysteriously drawn to travel to a castle in Spain, where he met several times with Fulcanelli, who appeared in good health despite his supposed age of between 110 and 120 years. Early one morning during this visit, Canseliet encountered a group of women in sixteenth-century garb. As the shy alchemist beat a hasty retreat to his rooms, one of the women suddenly turned around and looked him in the eye. Beyond a shadow of doubt, Canseliet said, the "woman" was his master Fulcanelli, who had clearly transcended the duality of gender.

Such accounts reflect what many have called the Western ideal of androgyny, a melding in one individual of masculine (in Greek, *andro)* and feminine *(gyn)* values. Androgyny has ancient roots. The Christian Gnostics, for instance, believed not only that humans descended from a single androgynous being but that they return to that form after death. In the Gnostic *Gospel of Thomas,* Jesus says to his disciples, "And when you make the inner as the outer, and the outer as the inner, and the upper as the lower, and when you make male and female into a single one, so that the male shall not be male and the female shall not be female, then shall you enter the Kingdom."

Another believer in the importance of recognizing the masculine and feminine within each psyche was the Swiss psychiatrist Carl Jung, a protégé of Freud's who later broke with the master over metaphysical issues. While pondering the matter of androgyny, Jung developed the concepts of *anima,* the unconscious feminine element that exists in the male psyche, and *animus,* the unconscious masculine soul of the female psyche.

In his own personal life, the anima was very real, a feminine voice that spoke to him directly for many years. "It is she who communicates the images of the unconscious to the conscious mind," Jung wrote in his 1962 book *Memories, Dreams, Reflections,* "and that is what I chiefly valued her for. For decades I always turned to the anima when I felt that my emotional behavior was disturbed, and that something had been constellated in the unconscious. I would then ask the anima: 'Now what are you up to? What do you see? I should like to know.' After some resistance she regularly produced an image. As soon as the image was there, the unrest or the sense of oppression vanished."

For lay seekers, such a celebration of one's inner male and female qualities continues to hold a mystical allure as a powerful means of self-discovery. "A secret knowledge belongs to the androgyne," psychoanalyst and New Age author June Singer has written. "One learns to recognize the inner oscillation of Masculine and Feminine . . . and to hear with the inner ear the music of their interplay."

Driving the Devil Out

For many people, possession by a malevolent spirit is a real and frightening possibility. Typically, a demon is thought to invade the body of an innocent human being and then use that person for the devil's work. Many cultures have developed rituals to rid the possessed of these evil spirits; among the best known exorcism rites is that of the Catholic church.

An account of one twentieth-century case of possession and exorcism—based on the vivid documentation of those who witnessed it—is presented on these pages. It involved a South African adolescent named Clara Germana Celle *(above)*, who attended school and church at Saint Michael's, a mission near Durban. Her teachers found the girl intelligent, kind, and honest; although she could be moody and excitable, Germana was respectful toward the priests and nuns. In her sixteenth year, however, she began refusing to take communion, and, reportedly, everyone noticed a strange glitter in her eyes.

On July 5, 1906, after questioning by Father Erasmus Hoerner, her spiritual mentor, Germana was said to reluctantly hand over a paper on which was written a pact with the devil. Ten days later, while Father Erasmus was away visiting another mission, the young woman suddenly became distraught, screaming, "I am lost! I have lied in confession and taken communion in an impure state. I must hang myself. Satan calls me!" Her teachers were understandably alarmed and the other students bewildered by her outburst. But that was only the beginning.

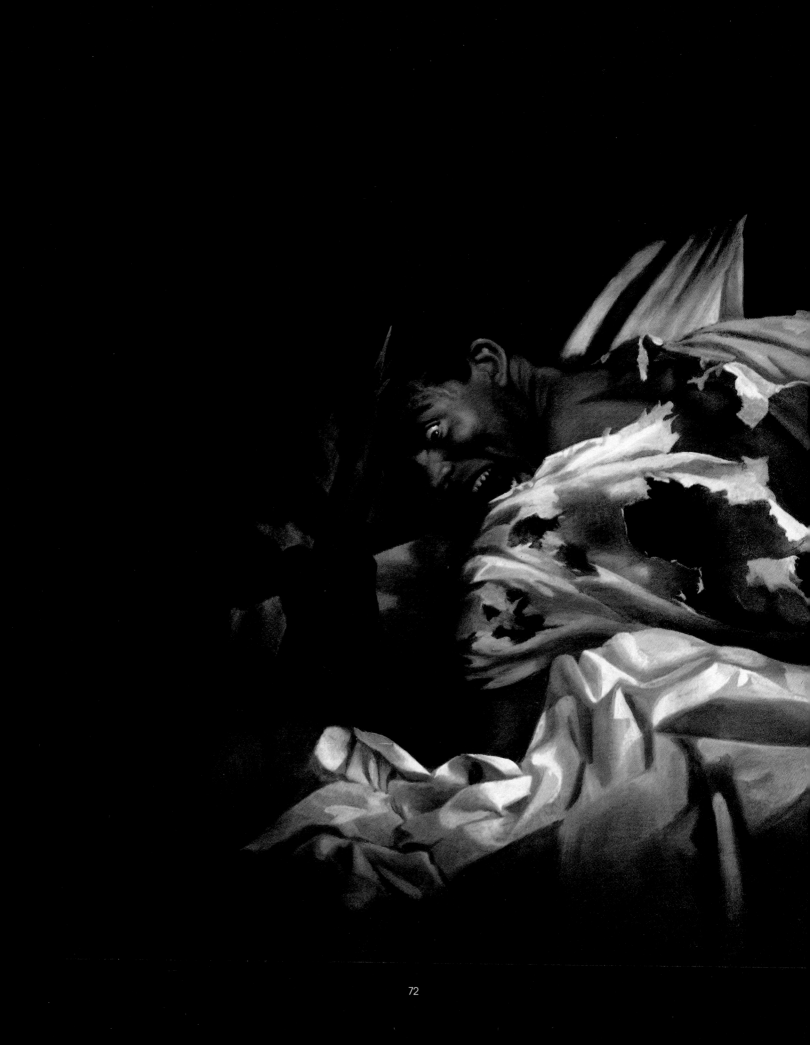

Over the next few weeks, Germana suffered other violent episodes. She seemed to argue with an unseen presence, and when she spoke her head jerked to one side. But the most frightening scene took place on August 20, when a nun found Germana thrashing wildly in her room. She was tearing her dress, growling and barking like a dog, and screaming for help. With extraordinary strength, the girl seized the bedpost and broke it, crying, "Sister, call Father Erasmus. I have to confess and tell everything."

When Father Erasmus arrived, he found Germana amid a cluster of schoolgirls and nuns, struggling as if in wild dispute with something invisible. Pointing to the priest, Germana pleaded with the unseen presence, "He has the note you wanted back. Ask him, he has it." The timbre of her voice abruptly changed, as if someone else were speaking. "Now our hour has come. Many will be sent from hell to torture and seduce you. Woe betide you, Germana!" Father Erasmus blessed the tormented girl and demanded, "Who are you?" From Germana's mouth came the words the priest had feared. "I am Satan."

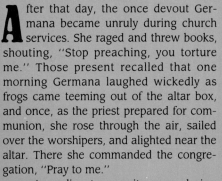

After that day, the once devout Germana became unruly during church services. She raged and threw books, shouting, "Stop preaching, you torture me." Those present recalled that one morning Germana laughed wickedly as frogs came teeming out of the altar box, and once, as the priest prepared for communion, she rose through the air, sailed over the worshipers, and alighted near the altar. There she commanded the congregation, "Pray to me."

According to eyewitnesses, during bouts of possession, Germana flinched from even carefully hidden holy medals and complained that holy water burned her skin. From her mouth came "a hellish choir" of "howling, barking, hissing, growling" noises, and her eyes "burned with an inhuman fire." She was suddenly fluent in Latin. She knew the secret sins of her schoolmates, and she knew instantly of events occurring at other missions. Father Erasmus, convinced that Germana was indeed possessed, petitioned the bishop for permission to perform an exorcism. The moment the request was signed, Germana knew that, too.

Starting in September, the mission community gathered for a total of four days to reclaim Germana's soul. She was calm at first, but as Father Erasmus recited the exorcism, she flailed violently and kicked the prayer book away. Her body became elastic, a second priest recalled, and "her neck elongated, so that it resembled a snake." In a flash, she struck a nun's arm, leaving teeth marks around "a small red wound like a snakebite." At one point, it took fifteen people to hold Germana down as she yelled, thrashed, and then floated off the floor. Even after being tied to her seat, the tormented girl levitated again, this time chair and all. Her body seemed pumped with air, the veins of her face swollen almost to bursting. Just when it appeared the strain had become too much for her, she issued a harrowing, woeful moan. Her body relaxed. It was over.

Germana told the priests that she had felt the demon leave her, that she was at peace and able to pray once more. After the exorcism, in the words of one priest, Germana "remained healed." She lived out her life at the mission and died just seven years later of tuberculosis.

CHAPTER 3

In the Grasp of Ageless Evil

kies over San Francisco were dark on the night of June 21, 1975, the eve of the summer solstice, a celestial event long favored by many religions for special ceremonies. In a chamber dimly lit by candles, a man draped in black stood before an altar on which were placed a bell, a candle, and a goblet. On the wall above, a silver pentagram glinted in the soft light. The solitary worshiper took the bell and rang it nine times as he slowly revolved in a counterclockwise circle. He then lit the candle on the altar and began an incantation: "In the name of Set, the Prince of Darkness, I enter into the Realm of Creation to work my Will upon the universe. . . ."

At that point, the celebrant later claimed, a second presence appeared in the room. He said that in the murky, flickering light he beheld a creature with the body of a man and the head of an antelope. The worshiper recognized this figure as the ancient Egyptian god Set, thought by some to be the earliest incarnation of what would one day be called Satan.

The midnight priest's name was Michael Aquino. He would later claim that on that dark June night Set anointed him the Second Beast—the leader who would rekindle a religion that had last flourished more than 5,000 years before. As a sign of his ascendancy, Aquino plucked his eyebrows into sharp upward angles, cropped his hair to a point on his forehead, and tattooed the Antichrist's number, 666, on his scalp. And before the year was out, the so-called Second Beast founded a modern-day Temple of Set.

In almost every respect, Michael Aquino's background seemed ill suited to his new vocation. A former Eagle Scout who held a Ph.D. in political science, Aquino had served in Vietnam as a lieutenant in Army Intelligence. He became intrigued by Satanism in 1969, after attending a lecture by Anton Szandor La Vey, founder of the Church of Satan. In time, Aquino became a wholehearted convert to the religion, although he eventually broke with the Church of Satan over political and philosophical differences.

Unlike La Vey, who claimed he was only symbolically worshiping Satan, Aquino insisted that he was worshiping a real being, not a mere representation of evil. Aquino believed that Satan was an intelligent entity in conflict with the laws of the universe, and that all of humanity had an unrealized potential to view the world from Satan's perspective. Although he once pledged "to destroy the influence of conventional religion," Aquino claimed to abhor violence. Any member of his sect who was found sacrificing "any life form" was threatened with expulsion from the temple.

Despite his claim to a benign Satanism, he was investigated by San Francisco police in 1987 on suspicion of child molestation. Although no charges were filed, his apartment was ransacked. He sued the city for slander, calling the episode a "modern witch-hunt in the most classical sense." If, as Aquino contends, the police were harassing him because he chooses to worship a god of darkness forgotten for thousands of years, it could be said they were following an unwarranted tradition that dates back at least to medieval times. Surely, one could argue, Aquino's activities—however bizarre—were harmless. After all, in today's modern, highly scientific world, the notion of evil in the form of a grinning Satan and his minions seems patently absurd.

But in fact many thoughtful people find the idea of Satan worship more threatening than amusing. Moreover, in this era of world wars, terrorism, and increasingly violent crime, human beings can hardly claim to have conquered evil. Much has already been learned about human behavior, yet society remains bewildered, often helpless, in the face of the cruel acts people inflict on people.

From Satan to Adolf Hitler, each age finds its personification of evil. In Western culture, the notion of an otherworldly source of evil has been all but supplanted by modern sociological and psychological perspectives. Yet experience indicates that those who consciously claim to embrace malevolent forces often find a ready and rapidly expanding band of followers for their messages of hate, and evil that supposedly is purely spiritual too frequently takes physical expression in heinous deeds. Moreover, modern religious authority still recognizes spiritual evil as a harmful reality; even in such advanced cultures as those of North America and Western Europe, exorcisms of demons are still conducted under the auspices of mainstream religion. The persistence of such practices parallels an enduring popular belief in a supernatural source of evil—however enlightened we may believe our age and society to be.

Of all the forces at work in human history, none is more tenacious, or more difficult to comprehend, than evil. No person in any time or place has lived a life untouched by evil, yet its exact nature remains defiant of definition. Western philosophers commonly identify three kinds of evil: moral evil, or the deliberate imposition of suffering by one person on another; natural evil, as in the cases of disease and natural di-

Telltale hoofs, horns, and bat's wings reveal the devilish nature of this creature and similar ones on subsequent pages. Since biblical times, people have accused such demons—reportedly either fallen angels or the progeny of Adam and Lilith, Eve's evil predecessor—of wreaking havoc on earth.

sasters; and metaphysical evil, defined as the inherent imperfections of the world as we know it. Other cultures have defined evil in many different ways. Some American Indian tribes consider vice, pollution, and even simple misfortune to be evil. Muslims say pride and opposition to God are the ultimate evils. In ancient Egypt, anything that violated the cosmic order was deemed inherently bad. And of course in the grand scheme of cosmic duality, evil may be defined as the opposite force that balances the power of good—whatever good might be.

Although they may be hard pressed to explain it, most people think they know evil when they see it. The greatest difficulty in this, however, is that humans tend to see only the evil that others do. How simple it would be, wrote Alexander Solzhenitsyn, the Nobel Prize-winning author who survived Stalin's concentration camps, "if only there were evil people somewhere insidiously committing evil deeds, and it were necessary only to separate them from the rest of us and destroy them. But the line dividing good and evil cuts through the heart of every human being. And who is willing to destroy a piece of his own heart?"

If humans have had trouble defining evil through the ages, they have had no difficulty giving it names and faces—Satan, Lucifer, Beelzebub, Mephistopheles, the Tempter,

the Evil One, the Prince of This World, the Prince of Demons. The lexicon of evil spans a thousand names in every language on earth, back to the beginning of human time.

Searching for supernatural explanations for suffering and death, the earliest religions tended to view their gods in terms of the conflict between good and evil. The Egyptian god Seth, for example, was the god of the desert, in constant battle with Horus, the god of the fertile Nile region. Although Seth was associated with infertility and destruction, he was never directly equated with evil—even though he and Set, the Egyptian deity Michael Aquino claims to have summoned up, share certain characteristics. Instead the Egyptians saw evil in the constant struggle between Horus and Seth and sought to reconcile the two opposing principles. In some writings Seth and Horus are one god.

This powerful tension between good and evil in a single personification is also seen in the Hindu gods Vishnu and Shiva. Both are creators and destroyers of life, but neither is considered evil by enlightened Hindus. Likewise, Tibetan Buddhism has its share of seemingly wrathful deities. Some are depicted holding hats brimful with blood; others display sharp fangs. As devilish as some of these creatures seem, they stand for subtle virtues that human beings often fail to recognize as noble.

The cosmic dualism of the struggle between forces of good and evil was played out more clearly in Christianity and its Hebraic forebear. The original Hebrew God also embodied both good and evil. But as Jews repeatedly suffered outrageous persecution, they came to doubt that their God could inflict such pain upon them. Thus the idea of a separate, distinct embodiment of evil began to make its way into Hebrew thought.

Some scholars credit another cause for the change in belief. Near the beginning of the sixth century BC, the Jews were carried off in bondage to Babylon. After several decades of exile there, they

Satanic priest Anton Szandor La Vey looms balefully from the darkness in this 1970s portrait. Founder of the Church of Satan in San Francisco, he has taught his followers to accept and glorify the seamy side of human nature, celebrating indulgence, lust, vengeance, and greed.

were freed by the Persian king Cyrus the Great, who conquered the Babylonians. The Persian religion Zoroastrianism was strikingly dualistic. A benevolent god, Ohrmazd, opposed an evil one, Ahriman. The Jews' belief in an evil figure appears to date from around the time of their return to Israel from Persian-ruled Babylon. From the Persians, too, they seemed to have acquired the concept of a dualistic afterlife—heaven for those who merited it and hell for people who led evil lives. Previously, Hebraic writings spoke of a single afterlife, Sheol, a dark underworld that awaited all who died, whether their lives had been good or bad.

Satan, Hebrew for "adversary," was originally depicted as God's prosecutor, an angel who tested and judged believers. But he apparently grew arrogant, once afflicting the righteous Job with a debilitating skin disease simply to test a point about the frailty of human faith. Christians inherited much of Hebrew religious thought, and by the time of the early Christian Scriptures, Satan had gone too far. As Lucifer (Roman for "morning star"), he was cast from heaven for his overweening pride. Although God remained in charge, the devil had been born and was eager for his due.

But a disturbing question arose: Was Satan simply a pawn in God's game, or an independent force? In the second century of Christianity, this problem was pondered by a dissident sect known as Gnostics. They believed in a radically dualistic universe, in which good was equated with the spiritual realm and stood in opposition to evil, incarnate in the material world. In the Gnostic gospel, the devil ruled the material world—including one's own flesh, described as "a wretched prison constructed by Satan to incarcerate the soul." Indeed, the Gnostics were so opposed to the physical world that they condemned the God of the Old Testament for having created it.

Gnostics were a secretive, mysteri-ous lot. There is some evidence that a few Gnostics did in fact engage in loathsome practices—even cannibalism—as extreme demonstrations of the worthlessness of earthly existence. The official life of Gnosticism was short; the original sect died out sometime in the fourth century. But by upending many cherished Judeo-Christian principles, Gnostics anticipated the development of modern Satanism.

While other religions were rife with evil spirits, Christianity developed a veritable army of demons under Lucifer's generalship. In the late second and early third centuries, the Christian scholar Origen created an entire "diabology," an elaborate survey of evil. Origen believed that moral goodness required freedom of choice, and he proposed the idea that God created intelligent beings free to make the choice between good and evil. Having reached their decisions, these beings emerged as angels, humans, or sometimes as underworld demons. According to Origen, the number of these souls was fixed, but each could rise and fall—an angel might sink to demonhood, and Satan could well rise to angelhood. Origen himself believed that Satan would eventually be saved and that all souls would in time return to God and melt into his perfect unity.

Early monks saw themselves as foot soldiers in the war between good and evil. These holy hermits lived spare lives away from the distractions of society, often in the desert, where Satan had tempted their master, Jesus.

The model for all monks who came after him was Saint Antony, the ascetic spiritual leader who lived between AD 251 and 356. According to later accounts of his life, this holy man endured numerous encounters with Satan, who tempted him with everything from wealth to a less burdensome life. When temptation failed, the devil reportedly conjured a host of terrors. Once Antony awoke from a sound sleep to confront a menagerie of

While the lead character in the 1945 film The Picture of Dorian Gray retains youthful beauty, his portrait decays, revealing the corruption of his soul.

leopards, scorpions, and snakes that had overrun his bedchamber. Finally the devil himself appeared in his most fearsome form. "In his mouth gape burning lamps," Antony related. "The smoke of a furnace blazing with the fire of coals flares from his nostrils."

Although Antony resisted the devil's blandishments and threats, the power of evil arose again and again to tempt those who followed him. If monks were not safe from the devil, everyday Christians were thought to be in constant jeopardy. As a result, the religion grew more formal and codified, and anyone who failed to adhere strictly to the Church's teachings was considered a heretic. In time, these stragglers from the path came to be identified with Satanic worship. In 1022, King Robert of France ordered the first Christian execution of heretics. Some of the supposed sinners attempted to defend themselves in court, but their suggestion that God might have a rival in Satan proved explosive. Pious Frenchmen tried to storm the trial and lynch the heretics, who were eventually burned at the stake anyway.

Despite the horrifying punishments awaiting those convicted of consorting with the so-called Evil One, there were people in those dark ages who, because of the bleak circumstances of their lives, felt compelled to approach the devil for assistance. The Luciferans of the thirteenth century were said to secretly worship Satan as the unjustly disenfranchised brother of God. Their rebellion led them to disdain the traditions of the Church and to show their contempt for Christ. When they took Holy Communion at Easter, for example, they would surreptitiously keep the wafers in their mouths; after leaving church, they would spit them into the sewer. Such behavior did not go unpunished; inquisitors managed to wring a full confession out of one Luciferan adherent.

The fear of devil worship, and the persecution of suspected devil worshipers, reached its height between 1450 and 1750, when as many as three million people in Europe and colonial America were branded as witches and executed for consorting with the devil. A book called *The Hammer of Witches,* written by two inquisitors in 1486, helped to fuel the craze; it was said to rival the Bible as a bestseller. The so-called science of demonology grew to be so elaborate that at one point no fewer than 7,405,926 demons, of every imaginable type and degree of evil, were identified. Persecution of suspected witches was cruel. On the theory that consorting with the devil left telltale marks on the body, seventeenth-century inquisitors used long needles called bodkins to probe each blemish on a suspect's skin. Since devil's marks were said to be impervious to pain, the inquisitor would plunge the bodkin into every mole, wart, and pimple—often straight through to the bone—testing for unresponsiveness. The suspects' cries of anguish usually fell on deaf ears.

Apparently even the pure in spirit were sometimes caught in a wily demon's grasp. Some evil beings were said to mate with innocent men and women in their sleep. A seductive male demon, called an incubus, allegedly prowled convents at night in search of nuns to defile. These lustful creatures sometimes proved a convenient scapegoat for demons of another type: When a medieval nun claimed to have been sexually molested by one Bishop Silvanus, the good bishop had a ready explanation—the sister, he insisted, had been victimized by an incubus disguised as himself. Malformed babies—and even twins—were thought to be the offspring of such unholy unions.

The female counterpart to an incubus was a succubus. "There were places," claimed the eleventh-century saint Albertus Magnus, "in which a man can scarcely sleep at night without a succubus accosting him." While the price of willingly sleeping with a succubus was eternal damnation, the thought proved titillating to some. A resourceful brothel keeper in Bologna, said to have "staffed his entire establishment with succubi," apparently found an eager clientele.

With the rise in Europe of ecclesiastical courts, intercourse with the devil began to take a legalistic turn. Now, it was said, a sinner clinched a relationship with the devil through a contract signed in blood. History's most infamous pact with the devil was signed by the legendary Faust, a mythological figure whose grim story has inspired great works of literature, art, and music.

The legend was first widely circulated in 1587, with the publication of Johann Spiess's *Historia von Dr. Johann Faustus*. According to Spiess, the story began on a dark night, when the young Faust, a student of philosophy, crept to a deserted crossroads, drew a magic circle, and dared to summon the devil. A burning orb rose from the ground. As Faust gaped in wonder, the orb transformed into various shapes—first a dragon, then a man on fire, and finally a figure in the robes of a Catholic friar. In this final, irreverent form, the figure introduced itself to the shaken Faust as Lucifer's messenger, Mephistopheles.

Mephistopheles, in a much more subtle style than his evil predecessors, persuaded Faust to sign a pact in which he would receive twenty-four years of supernatural services in return for his soul. The remainder of Faust's life passed quickly as his thirst for knowledge gave way to every variety of sin. In a blur of unholy debauchery, Faust satisfied his lusts with whores and succubi; mocked the world's emperors, holy men, and professors; and gorged himself continually on food, drink, and even, at one point, on a bale of hay. When the day came to meet his fate, a suddenly repentant Faust gave a sermon to his friends warning against the path he had taken.

But it was too late. At the stroke of midnight, a whirlwind encircled his house, and a long, hopeless scream pierced the night air. At dawn, all that remained of the unfortunate Faust was a hideously mangled corpse, with its head brutally twisted all the way around to the back.

Through the years, the Faust myth retained a curious force. When England's Christopher Marlowe wrote his most famous play, *The Tragicall History of Doctor Faustus,* in the 1500s, its effect was so powerful that an actor named Edward Allyn, playing the title role, was said to have accidentally conjured up a real, brimstone-stinking devil on stage.

Few could mistake the ultimate message of Doctor Faustus: If in Christianity the devil embodied evil, hell was the sinner's ultimate destination—a belief that runs through most of the world's ancient cultures. The Greeks' Hades was an endlessly oppressive place where the great majority of the dead were deprived of light, happiness, and all the joys of life. Similarly, the Babylonian epic *Gilgamesh* described a world where the dead flew ceaselessly in the darkness with nothing to eat but clay and dust.

A woman dreams in sensual abandon as her nocturnal seducer, a leering incubus, perches on her breast in Henry Fuseli's 1781 painting, The Nightmare. Christian theologians once thought incubi and succubi—male and female lover-demons—lured those who were abstemious by day into erotic indulgence at night.

The ancient Egyptians may have been the first to describe an afterlife of rewards and punishments in their Book of the Dead. Among Hindus and Buddhists sin was equated with evil karma—the bad deeds of one's life—to be addressed if the soul was to advance to liberation and enlightenment. In the Tibetan Book of the Dead, the soul, after death, faced a mirror held by the terrifying Yama, king of the dead, and judged itself. The soul faced horrific punishment for its sins, but the punishment was self-inflicted.

In the Judeo-Christian tradition, the notion of hell as a fiery place had its origins, strangely enough, in a municipal dump. Gehenna, the pit where Jerusalem's trash was burned, came to represent a place of hellfire. By the second century AD, hell had become an immensely more complex realm. It was described in chilling detail in the *Apocalypse of Peter*, one book in a body of works now known as apocalyptic literature. Written over a span of time—from about 200 BC to AD 350—these texts aimed to resolve the conflicts that arose from contemplating the righteousness of God and the suffering of his righteous children on earth.

Peter describes visions in which Christ shows him the torments of hell: "And some were there hanging by their tongues; and these were they that blasphemed the way of righteousness, and under them was laid fire flaming and tormenting them. . . . And there were also others, women hanged by their hair above the mire which boiled up; and these were they that adorned themselves for adultery. . . . And in another place were gravel-stones sharper than swords or any spit, heated with fire, and men and women clad in filthy rags rolled upon them in torment. And these were they that were rich and trusted in their riches. . . ." Peter's terrifying portrait of hell has survived largely unchanged through millennia of Christian history. The histrionic, fire-and-brimstone pronouncements of modern evangelical preachers derive their power from this ageless vision.

Almost as fearsome as eternal damnation is the threat of demonic possession by an evil spirit during one's lifetime. Possession of an individual by spirits, demons, or other alien entities has often been claimed by victims willing and unwilling and by spirits both hostile and benevolent. In one form or another, spirit possession has been reported in nearly every region of the world. A 1973 scientific survey of 488 societies found that roughly half of them have knowledge of "altered states of consciousness," which they attribute to spirit possession.

Possession is common in the practice of voodoo (from *vodun*, in the West African language of Fon, meaning "spirit" or "sacred object"). A religion often associated with Haiti, voodoo is also practiced throughout the Caribbean, Brazil, and the southern United States. Through its association with the feared and despised Tonton Macoute, the secret police of Haiti's deposed Duvalier regime, voodoo has earned a bad name. But its roots are found in an admixture of the traditional religion of Dahomey, a kingdom on the old Slave Coast of West Africa, and colonial Catholicism.

In voodoo, a person's soul, or *'ti bon ange* (little good angel), is lightly tethered to the body by the *gros bon ange* (large good angel). This fragile bond can easily be broken, by either catastrophe or magic. The result is a sort of living corpse, or zombie. Outside observers have described this phenomenon as a dissociated personality, in a state akin to daydreaming. In voodoo possession, however, the daydream becomes unshakeable. In this state people exhibit astonishing powers, such as walking on hot coals in bare feet, or display extraordinary strength and endurance.

The voodoo soul is highly susceptible to such dissociation. A woman can make a man fall in love with her by serving him a meal in which she has mixed her own fingernail clippings. Haitian men who have eaten food they suspect has been tainted by an enemy will supposedly vomit lizards and centipedes. People often come to the voodoo faith in order to be relieved of the fear of dissociation; voodoo teaches them how to embrace the experience as a positive one. Through elaborate dances and chanted rituals, adherents actu-

ally induce a trancelike possession by spirits called *loas,* most of which are considered benevolent.

A person possessed in a voodoo ceremony is said to be mounted by a loa. In 1947, a Western filmmaker named Maya Deren was filming a Haitian voodoo dance when she found herself suddenly mounted by a loa known as Erzulie—or so she later reported. "To be precise," she wrote, "I must call it a white darkness, its whiteness a glory and its darkness terror. It is the terror which is the greater force. . . . The white darkness moves up the veins of my leg like a swift tide rising . . . which, surely, will burst my skin. . . . 'Mercy!' I scream within me. I hear it echoed by the voices shrill and unearthly, 'Erzulie.' The bright darkness floods up through my body, reaches my head, engulfs me. I am sucked down and exploded upward at once."

Ioan Lewis, a professor at the London School of Economics, studied similar cases of possession in Africa's Somali Republic. In this Muslim society, illness and emotional upheaval are attributed to *zar,* greedy demons who inhabit people in order to gain access to rich foods and other finer things in life. The Somali women, who have little power and are frequently neglected by their husbands, can achieve a more exalted status through zar possession. Zar possession will occur, for example, when a husband announces his intention of taking a second wife. The cure for such a possession is an expensive exorcism, the cost of which may curb a husband's wandering eye.

The Christian faith, too, boasts its share of fearsome possessions. Since the Old Testament's Saul endured seizures caused by an evil spirit dispatched by Yahweh, many forms of physical and mental illness have been attributed to hateful demons. Fourteenth- and fifteenth-century Europeans recorded hundreds of supposed cases of possession and exhaustively cataloged their symptoms. The face of the possessed was said to warp into the features of the devil. The body grew thin and the stomach bloated. Black breath and vomiting were common, as was internal pain "like an animal eating the entrails." The possessed suffered convulsions, bellowed obscenities

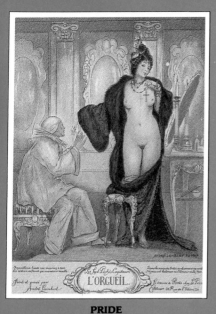

PRIDE

ENVY

ANGER

SLOTH

AVARICE

GLUTTONY

To devout Christians, the seven deadly sins—portrayed here in sensuous 1918 prints by French artist André Lambert—neatly summarize the force of evil as it manifests itself in human beings. Initially defined in fourth-century Christian Egypt, the sins—pride, envy, anger, sloth, avarice, gluttony, and lust—are thought to perpetuate the world's ills. The consequences of committing any of them—and thus furthering evil on earth—are dire: The Church traditionally has taught that unrepentant transgressors create so great a rift between themselves and God that the

LUST

Deity withholds from them the promise of eternal life.

Each of the deadly sins compromises human performance of good works. People guilty of pride worship themselves rather than serving God. Envious men and women delight in the misfortune and despise the success of other people. Anger leads to hurtful speech and actions, and through sloth, people ignore God-given opportunity. Material wealth ranks above God for the avaricious, as do food and drink for gluttons. And lustful men and women trade the path of righteousness for fleshly pleasures.

in unnaturally deep voices, and projected a freezing cold aura.

If possession is a venerable tradition in Christianity, so too is its cure, exorcism. Throughout early Christianity the ability of a devout follower, ordained or otherwise, to perform exorcisms was a sign of God's grace. Jesus exorcised demons, and the clothes of the apostle Paul were draped on the possessed and diseased to rid them of evil spirits. In today's Catholic church, however, the rites of exorcism are no longer part of the basic curriculum for would-be priests; only those who take special instruction may conduct exorcisms.

In exorcism, the cosmic struggle between good and evil is played out between priest and evil spirit on the battleground of the possessed. As the demon fights to stay in its victim, the priest invokes the name of Jesus to drive it out. According to a fourth-century account of an exorcism in Verona, the ritual took its toll on the possessed: "But as soon as we enter into the field of divine combat and begin to drive them forth with the arrow of the holy name of Jesus, then thou mayest take pity on the [possessed]. His face is suddenly deprived of color, his body rises up of itself, the eyes in madness roll in their sockets and squint horribly, the teeth, covered with a horrible foam, grind between blue-white lips; the limbs twisted in all directions are given over to trembling; he sighs, he weeps."

Such horrific symptoms manifested themselves in a celebrated case that began in 1865 in the German town of

Fantastic fanged reptiles, coiling vipers, and licking flames torment the damned in The Inferno, a nightmarish, door-spanning mural painted in 1825 by Tyrolean artist Joseph Anton Koch. The artist drew upon Dante's epic poem of the same title to create this chilling vision of the fate of sinners.

Illfurth. The ordeal, which lasted four years, began without warning as a pair of brothers—Theobald, age ten, and Josef, age seven—suddenly began to exhibit frightening and repulsive signs of demon possession. Their bodies swelled and sometimes levitated mysteriously above their beds. They suffered from hideous infestations of lice and vermin. On occasion, after complaining of a painful itching, the boys reached beneath their clothing to produce handfuls of foul-smelling seaweed and feathers.

Often, their room grew unbearably hot, although it was not heated by a stove or fire. Only when their mother sprinkled holy water on the bed would the room return to a normal temperature. Indeed, holy water, rosaries, and other

children were said to show great delight. "That is one of ours," they would cry, as if in triumph. "They should all be like that!"

As the months wore on, Theobald and Josef displayed previously unknown knowledge and talents. Both demonstrated a command of French, Latin, English, and Spanish—although prior to their possession they had spoken only their native German. And they began to exhibit a ghoulish talent for prophecy. Frequently Theobald would kneel on the edge of his bed and sweep his arms as though ringing a mourning bell. He would then solemnly predict the death of an acquaintance of the family. On one occasion, when the boy announced that he was tolling the death of a villager named Gregor Kunegel, the man's daughter happened to be standing nearby. The young woman reacted angrily. "You liar," she cried, "my father isn't even ill. He is working on the new boys' seminary building as a mason."

Theobald gave a chilling answer: "That may be, but he has just had a fall. Go ahead and check on it!" The boy's grim prediction proved true. At the precise moment that Theobald had begun his bell-ringing motions, Gregor Kunegel had fallen from a scaffold and snapped his neck.

By October of 1869, the local clergy of Illfurth admitted themselves to be powerless to help the boys. As a last resort, a Father Souquat was commissioned to perform an exorcism. It was decided that the brothers should be exorcised separately. First, Theobald was taken to a nearby chapel, where three strong men were needed to restrain him as the ritual began. The boy struggled, his eyes closed and his beet red lips swollen and distorted, and a thick stream of viscous yellow froth poured from his mouth. He bellowed furiously in a voice that reminded one listener of "a calf being strangled." Later, a straitjacket was used to keep him under control. After several days, the exorcism rites finally began to

sanctified objects drew a particularly strong reaction from the boys. "Whenever these were brought near," wrote one observer, "the two brothers began to act up violently. They foamed at the mouth and fought with all their strength against contact with these items. If a drop of holy water was mixed secretly with their food, they refused to touch it." Once, when offered a plate of figs that had been blessed by a priest, the boys flew into a rage. "Take these rat heads away," they shouted. "The fellow in the black suit has made faces over them!"

Whenever a priest visited the house, the brothers would hide underneath a table or the bed, or even jump out a window. But when a less devout individual paid a call, the

Exorcism the Catholic Way

Since time began, people have believed evil spirits could capture and manipulate individuals. Almost all societies have turned to exorcists—be they called shamans, priests, witch doctors, or other titles—to free those caught in the spells of demons.

A detailed exorcism ritual, the *Rituale Romanum,* was developed by the Catholic church in 1614 and is still occasionally performed. Before conducting an exorcism, a priest must be satisfied the candidate is truly possessed. During the Renaissance, such behavior as fear of the cross, emission of a vile stench, or fluency in previously unknown languages was considered proof. Today, demonic inhabitation is proclaimed only when doctors cannot find a medical or psychological explanation for mysterious symptoms.

At the start of an exorcism, the possessed person, or demoniac, sits in a church, restrained if violent. The priest wraps one end of his stole about the victim's shoulders as an expression of that person's inclusion in God's community. Sprinkling holy water, the exorcist solemnly recites prayers and reads from Scripture, makes the sign of the cross, and lays a hand or a cross on the victim's head *(right).* The priest then commands the demon to leave: "I exorcise thee, most vile spirit, to get out and flee from this creature of God." He shouts epithets—"foe to the human race, producer of death"—to discourage the fiend. The evil spirit is thought to flee the demoniac in terrified recognition of the supremacy of the forces of light. If a total cure is not effected by the exorcism, the Church states that possession was a misdiagnosis.

have an effect. Throwing his head back, Theobald gave one last furious roar. Then he fell into a deep sleep. When he awoke, the boy had no recollection of the exorcism ceremony. Young Josef underwent a similar ordeal. For several hours the child screamed and struggled with unnatural strength, then he, too, collapsed into a deep sleep. Like his brother, Josef was amazed when he regained consciousness in a church, surrounded by strangers. Both boys at last appeared to be free of the evil spirits that had tormented them for four long years.

Regrettably, it is nearly impossible to weigh the accounts of the Illfurth possession against modern beliefs about exorcism. Many symptoms once considered sure signs of possession have been traced to specific diseases. A neurological disorder called Tourette's syndrome, for example, can cause people to shout obscenities, make animal noises, stamp their feet, and contort their faces in a fashion that might have rivaled the antics of the Illfurth boys.

For such reasons, the Catholic church now maintains that "genuine possession by discarnate spirits is accepted, in principle, as having occurred in the past, particularly as described in the gospels, but any specific modern instance is apt to be regarded as due to natural mental disease process."

Despite official efforts to consign exorcism to the past, the practice has persisted as a cure of last resort. Though controversial, exorcism appears to have had some benefit in a handful of contemporary cases. As Leslie Watkins, author of the 1983 book *The Real Exorcists,* wrote, "In those cases where exorcism appears to work without disastrous side-effects, the argument between the religionists and the behaviorists is purely aca-

Believing that evil spirits infest the vital fluid of his companion, an initiate into the West African religion that spawned voodoo sucks blood from the man's arm. The initiate has entered a drug-induced trance state that is thought to empower him to perform the exorcism.

demic. Even atheists would think it a sin to let someone continue to suffer the agony of serious mental disturbance rather than let a priest administer a cure.''

Unfortunately, some exorcisms have produced disastrous side effects. In 1976, a young woman named Anneliese Michel underwent exorcism in a little town in Bavaria. For years she had suffered excruciating ''molestations'' by some unknown entity, which caused pains, sleeplessness, and bizarre behavior. She broke crucifixes and once physically attacked an elderly priest. Doctors diagnosed her as epileptic, but her parents believed she was possessed. At their request, and with the apparent blessing of the young woman, the bishop of Würzburg, Dr. Josef Stangl, assigned the case to two priests, Father Renz and Father Alt.

The exorcism began on September 24, 1975. The ordeal, recorded on forty-two cassette tapes, was to last longer—and cause more heartbreak—than any of the participants could have imagined. Day after day of steady incantations by the priests produced a shocking response: The priests believed they found six evil spirits inhabiting Anneliese, including Cain, the son of Adam and Eve who jealously slew his brother Abel; Adolf Hitler, the leader of Nazi Germany responsible for the extermination of millions of people; Pastor Fleischmann, a fourteenth-century cleric who had beaten a man to death in his own parish; and finally Lucifer himself.

The long and torturous exorcism culminated on All Hallows' Eve, when Father Renz coaxed the offending spirits out of Anneliese's body one by one, forcing them to say a Hail Mary prayer as they were dispatched to the depths from which they had come. All of the known demons were supposedly drawn out; however, a seventh, unidentified evil spirit remained. Father Renz renewed his efforts, and the exorcism dragged on for several more months. By the following summer, Anneliese could no longer withstand the ordeal. At the age of twenty-three, having wasted away to skin and bones, the young woman died.

A local prosecutor immediately launched an investigation into Anneliese's death. It was discovered that no one involved had sought medical help for the woman, even though a doctor's intervention might have made the difference between life and death. Two years later, after a long and highly publicized review of the events, the priests and the woman's parents were brought to trial and convicted of negligent homicide. But the affair did not end there: The bishop who had sanctioned the exorcism died shortly after the verdicts were rendered—out of grief, according to his friends.

Contemporary cases of exorcism are, if anything, more numerous in America than in Europe. According to Malachi Martin, a former Jesuit professor and an authority on demon possession, 125 exorcisms were performed in the United States in 1975 alone. Martin details several case histories of possession in his 1976 book, *Hostage to the Devil: The Possession and Exorcism of Five Living Americans.* One describes the ordeal of a Father Peter—Martin chose not to reveal the priest's true identity—who in 1965 was asked to perform an exorcism on a twenty-six-year-old woman in New York City.

According to Martin, whether a priest succeeds or fails

in an attempted exorcism, he suffers, because in order to intercede for the possessed he must bare his own soul to the merciless lashings of the malignant spirit. This proved painfully true in Father Peter's case. The episode of the tormented young woman in New York was to be Father Peter's third exorcism, and his last.

The woman in question, known as Marianne, came from a devout Roman Catholic family, but she had a keen sense of life's duality—that the sunny side must inevitably be balanced by shadows. She felt that most people overemphasized the positive; this conviction, coupled with a rebellious streak, gave her a tendency to focus on the negative. When her schoolteachers and, later, her college professors tried to help her balance her views, she accused them of trying to enslave her mind. She chose instead to seek unadulterated reality, or, in her words, the "naked light."

As she continued her lonely quest, she began to notice a man who appeared with uncanny timing at critical moments of her life. One Palm Sunday, Marianne decided out of curiosity to venture into a church for the first time in a long while. During the service she was overcome with a sense of revulsion. The mysterious man appeared next to her, smiling, and said, "Had enough, my friend? The smile of the Kingdom is now yours." Or so she said.

Soon afterward, she found the man sitting on a bench in Manhattan's Bryant Park. As she sat down beside him, she felt an invisible net closing around her. "As the net contracted in size passing through my outer person," she later recalled, "it gathered and compressed every particle of my self." Then the pressure eased and Marianne found she had achieved the "thrill of balance" she had been seeking so long. "Don't fear," said her strange companion, "you have now married nothingness and are of the Kingdom."

By the time of that fateful meeting, Marianne's weight had dropped from 130 to 95 pounds. She rarely spoke and seemed emotionless—except at the sight of a crucifix, the sound of a church bell, or the mention of Jesus. These things made her quake with fear. Her health was failing. Her parents brought her home to live with them, but within months she was bedridden, incontinent, and incoherent; her face was frozen into a twisted smile. Doctors could find nothing clinically wrong. Visits by the parish priest roused her to extreme violence and hysterical abuse, even attempts at suicide. Her room had a foul odor, the door would bang open and shut seemingly of its own accord, and Marianne's belongings were often found inexplicably broken. In desperation, her family sought an exorcist.

The job fell to Father Peter, who consulted several doctors, including two psychiatrists, before deciding to proceed. His caution may have been due to reluctance to begin the task. During a previous exorcism, a voice had issued him a direct warning through the clenched jaws of the possessed: "You'll be back for more. And we will scorch the soul in you. Scorch it. You'll smell. Just like us! Third strike and you're out! Pig! Remember us!"

Despite this demonic warning and his own misgivings, Father Peter began the exorcism just past midnight on a Monday in October. He was joined by a fellow priest, two burly friends of the family, a doctor, and

Adolf Hitler befriends a toddler in this German postcard known as "A Child's Gaze." It was intended to confer on the Führer the trust and affection of an innocent child, an act many would consider as evil as any ascribed to Hitler's regime.

Marianne's father. The room had been stripped of everything but Marianne's bed, a small table, and a chest of drawers. The stench in the bedroom was so strong that the men were forced to stuff their noses with cotton.

While his assistants held Marianne down, Father Peter doused her with holy water, saying, "Marianne, creature of God, in the name of God who created you and of Jesus who saved you, I command you to hear my voice." At these words, Marianne jerked into a sitting position and let out a howl that one witness likened to that of a wolf being slowly disemboweled. So began a nineteen-hour ordeal. The battle of wills between Father Peter and what the priest identified as Marianne's possessing spirit, who called himself the Smiler, ran the gamut from the philosophical to the obscene. At one point, the Smiler played off Marianne's fascination with duality, chanting convoluted statements such as "the real is real because of the unreal" and "the clean, clean because of the unclean." At other times, the Smiler would launch into profane tirades, accusing the exorcist of every manner of perversion. Eventually, the chest of drawers began to rattle and move of its own accord, and holy water sprinkled on it hissed as if on a hot stove.

Father Peter kept up his attack until, in a crescendo of noise and violence—during which Marianne's clothes split open and red welts sprouted on her body—the Smiler at last seemed to depart. Exhausted, Father Peter fell unconscious to the floor, unaware until he was revived that the exorcism had been successful. Marianne soon recovered, but Father Peter did not. He lapsed into a kind of gentle reverie and died within a year, at the age of sixty-two.

Regardless of occasional instances such as those of a Marianne or an Anneliese Michel, the Western world has in recent centuries gradually shed the view of evil as a distinct, animate force. Even the devil has been described in increasingly human ways. While still deeply evil, the Satan of Milton's *Paradise Lost,* published in 1674, is portrayed as almost courageous in his refusal to be subjugated to the will of God. When the German writer Johann Wolfgang von Goethe reworked the Faust legend in the early nineteenth century, Faust appeared less a sinner than a symbol of humankind's search for wisdom.

As scientific knowledge waxed, Western infatuation with evil began to wane. Insanity came to be understood as disease, not possession. Protestants took to calling the devil a Catholic superstition. In 1859, with the publication of Darwin's *On the Origin of Species by Means of Natural Selection,* so-called sacred science was thought to have been firmly supplanted by real science, and evil—or at least the idea of evil as a supernatural personage—began to fade away.

Evil has been transformed in modern society from a distinct, almost palpable reality to a concept or representation of social ills, thought to be explainable in other ways. And yet evil itself has hardly vanished. The wars and atrocities of the twentieth century surpass any in history.

Some people blame such horrors on the decline of religion with its moral strictures. Critics of pervasive secular opinion hold that the greatest danger of defining evil as abstract speculation is that people will begin to ignore the subject altogether. "The Devil's cleverest wile," wrote the French poet Baudelaire, "is to convince us that he does not exist." If secular views have lulled humankind into complacency in the twentieth century, nothing could have lent more credence to Baudelaire's statement than the rise of fascism, and particularly nazism.

The Nazis not only brought about an enormously tragic world war through geopolitical zealotry, but their mass extermination of Jews—combined with the apparent reluctance of the Allies to take action—embodied, to many, a paradigm of modern evil. However the atrocities came to pass, it seems clear that nazism served not only as an ideology but in many ways as a powerful religion for millions of Germans. At the Nazi party rally at Nuremberg in 1937, there hung an enormous picture of Adolf Hitler with an inscription that read, "In the beginning was the Word. . . ." A visitor to Germany in the late 1930s was informed by the mayor of the city of Hamburg that Germans needed no clergymen—they

were able to communicate with God through Hitler himself.

Theories about the religious antecedents and psychological causes of nazism are myriad. Based on knowledge that the infamous SS chief Heinrich Himmler was fascinated by the occult, some have proposed that the Nazi elite harked back to second-century Gnosticism and its inversion of Christian principles. Others believe that nazism gave the German masses a means of directing repressed sexual energy. Most analysts are careful to acknowledge a complex mixture of factors. However, one explanation that seems valid to psychologists and theologians alike was given by Adolf Hitler himself: "Those who see in National Socialism nothing more than a political movement know scarcely anything of it. It is more even than a religion: it is the will to create mankind anew."

In an effort to understand nazism and other seemingly inexplicable evils of the current age, many philosophers and psychologists have delved into the realm of the human subconscious—the dark, unexplored side of the psyche that may help to explain how seemingly ordinary people can become passive allies of evil.

A widely publicized 1971 psychological study by Philip Zimbardo of Stanford University indicated that the "dark side" of the human psyche can be unleashed when a person is put in a position of complete authority. For his experiment, Zimbardo transformed the basement of the Stanford University psychology building into a mock prison. Volunteers were solicited in a newspaper advertisement, and twenty-one respondents, most of them middle-class college students, were selected on the basis of their physical and mental stability. Half of the volunteers were assigned to be "prisoners" and half "guards." The prisoners were strip-searched, deloused, and issued prison clothes. The guards were told to "maintain a reasonable degree of order within the prison," although physical violence was forbidden.

The experiment was meant to last for two weeks. On the first day, however, one prisoner became so hysterical that he had to be released. Two days into the experiment, the rest of the prisoners staged a revolt, barricading them-

selves in their cells and hurling abuse at the guards. The guards responded fiercely, becoming cruel and sadistic, harassing and bullying the prisoners into submission. On day four, two more prisoners were released after showing signs of severe emotional disturbance. The guards, meanwhile, seemed to relish their power more and more. After only six days, an alarmed Zimbardo was forced to cancel the exercise. The aborted experiment, in the opinion of Zimbardo himself, had demonstrated "the power of social, institutional forces to make good men engage in evil deeds."

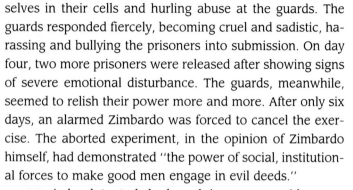

imbardo's study had much in common with an experiment conducted by Stanley Milgram at Yale University from 1960 to 1963, designed to assess a person's willingness to obey authority. Milgram's volunteers were told that they would be participating in a study of the effects of punishment on learning and memory. They were divided into "subjects" and "learners." The experimenter, an imposing figure in a lab coat, instructed the subjects to administer an electric shock to the learners whenever they gave wrong answers to a series of questions. For each wrong answer, the subjects were ordered to increase the voltage. There were thirty switches available to the subjects, starting at 15 volts and going up to 450 volts. The voltages were labeled in a range from Slight Shock to Intense Shock to Danger: Severe Shock. The final two switches were marked XXX.

Unbeknown to the subjects, the learners received no shocks at all; they merely acted the role. At 150 volts, the subjects heard them beg to be released from the experiment; at 270 volts, the learners began to scream as if in agony. If and when the subjects themselves asked to be excused from the study, the experimenter told them sternly that they had to continue.

A group of psychiatrists had predicted that only 3.73 percent of the subjects would obey the experimenter up to the 300-volt level, and that one in a thousand would apply maximum voltage. In reality, 62 percent of Milgram's subjects obeyed the experimenter all the way to the maximum 450 volts. In other words, the majority were willing to ad-

minister a potentially lethal dose of electricity to a fellow human being, simply on the order of an authority figure.

The eagerness with which so many seem to submit themselves and their actions to a higher authority—whether a person, an organization, or an ideology—may be a way of reducing the burden of personal responsibility. Stanley Milgram told his subjects that he would assume responsibility for any injury to the learners. Adolf Hitler and Heinrich Himmler had said as much to their German compatriots.

Unfortunately, such disturbing revelations are not confined to laboratory settings. A similar diffusion of responsibility has occurred in the mass society of the late twentieth century, leading to discontent among many and to a desperate search for direction among a few. "The average American is the incredible shrinking man," writes Arthur Lyons in his 1988 study of devil-worshiping cults, *Satan Wants You.* "There is nothing unique or powerful about him; he is just part of the herd, performing meaningless tasks, bored by his job." Lyons points to a resurgence of interest in mysticism and magic in the 1980s as a response to the breakdown of religious and moral codes, a way for some to displace the frustrations and anonymity of life in the technological age with a sense of power and fulfillment.

Perhaps it is not surprising, then, that the activities of Satanic cults have reportedly been on the rise in recent years, resulting in a heated national controversy. In numerous reports of the abduction, torture, and sacrifice of children by Satanic cults, the so-called survivors of these rituals have regularly come forward to tell their stories in print, on the lecture circuit, and on popular television shows.

One famous case was that of Michelle Smith, a Canadian woman who, during psychoanalysis, told a bizarre tale. Her mother, she said, had given her over to a Satanic cult at the age of five. There the young girl had allegedly been tortured physically and mentally for months; she even claimed to have seen the "Dark Prince" himself in the fires of the Black Mass. Her story, coauthored with her psychiatrist, Dr. Larry Pazder, earned large advances from book publishers and may have spurred other such "survivors" to come forward with their own tales.

According to Anson Shupe, a professor of sociology at Indiana University-Purdue University at Fort Wayne and an authority on the Satanic cult phenomenon, such confessions—legitimate or not—have led to a "Satanism-exposure-mania" that has become "a growth industry in this country." He cites a burgeoning group of self-proclaimed experts who traverse the United States offering training

A mask of the Satanists' evil lord, the devil's hood at right shrouds a mystery participant in a diabolic ceremony. Another trapping of Satanism, which relies heavily upon ritual and imagery to heighten the spiritual experience of belief, is the icon shown in the inset. This symbol mocks white magic by inverting its cherished pentagram and inscribing it with the face of a goat, one of the devil's favorite symbols.

workshops to local law-enforcement agencies, social-service workers, medical personnel, clergy, and educators. Commanding considerable sums for their appearances, these speakers, according to Shupe, "purport to reveal the rituals, implements, beliefs, symbols, and secret codes used by Satan's occult underground." From a scholarly standpoint, he considers "most of these seminars pure rubbish . . . a naive mishmash of occult and mystical traditions confused with shamanism and theatrical antics." J. Gordon Melton, director of the Institute for the Study of American Religion in Santa Barbara, California, agrees. "If what was being taught in these 'limited seminars' were revealed and became fair game for public discourse," he contends, "the ridiculousness of it would be evident."

For all the publicity that is given to the modern Satanic cults, there appears to be no growing, cohesive church of Satan. Michael Aquino's Temple of Set, though widely known through newspaper and television accounts, claims only some 100 adherents. Its larger rival, the San Francisco-based Church of Satan, founded by former lion tamer and police photographer Anton La Vey, boasts of "hundreds of thousands of members worldwide." However, in investigating the group for his 1989 book, *The Edge of Evil,* author Jerry Johnston found the Church of Satan to be "barely active two decades after its founding." And according to Cardinal John O'Connor, there were just two exorcisms performed in the entire New York archdiocese in 1989—a further indication, perhaps, that demonic possession has been on the decline.

Even if very few are committed to Satan, a remarkable number of people are willing to concede his existence. A 1990 Gallup poll revealed that 55 percent of adult Americans believed in the existence of Satan, and that an astonishing one in every ten actually claimed to have spoken with him. And there is little doubt, especially among law-enforcement officials, that involvement in Satanism can

have devastating effects—particularly on those who may already be mentally disturbed. A chilling case is that of Oklahoma teenager Sean Sellers. In 1983, depressed over a breakup with his girlfriend, Sellers had taken to drugs and "dedicated his life to Satan." Much of his dedication was expressed through attempts to shock others. He surrounded himself with the paraphernalia of devil worship and carried vials of his own blood to school and drank them in the cafeteria. Finally, overwhelmed by adolescent rage and alienation—and after long periods of sleeplessness and blackouts caused by drugs and alcohol—Sean Sellers murdered his mother, his stepfather, and a convenience-store clerk. For these crimes, he was sentenced to death in 1986.

In response to such episodes, Chicago's Hartgrove Hospital has established the Center for the Treatment of Ritualistic Deviance, specifically to help emotionally disturbed teenagers overcome their involvement with Satanism and its trappings. The patient profile, according to one of the staff psychologists, is of an intelligent, often creative teenager who feels bored and powerless, and who may look at Satanism—with its ritual use of drugs and focus on carnal pleasures—as a means to achieve an otherwise absent sense of power and excitement.

The success of such facilities remains to be seen, for without question the force of evil is the least understood element of humankind's collective psyche. Yet, to comprehend the delicate balance of human nature, one must struggle to understand the dark side as well as the bright. Too often, people are reluctant to acknowledge any degree of evil in themselves, their beliefs, and their actions. Too often, in their efforts to suppress or deny these dark forces, human beings fall prey to them. In the words of Henry Fairlie, author of the 1978 book *The Seven Deadly Sins Today,* "If we do not take seriously our capacity for evil, we are unable to take seriously our capacity for good."

A gaping-mouthed skull seems to laugh from the altar at the Church of Satan, as if to remind worshipers of their mortality. To its right lies a golden-bulbed aspergillum, a tool Catholics use at mass to sprinkle holy water. Satanists bastardize its sacred Christian function by filling it with human semen.

Paths of Righteousness

Easy is the descent to hell, wrote the first-century-BC poet Virgil, "but to withdraw, to make a way out to the upper air, that is the labour." In many cultures, refusing the temptations of evil and struggling to attain a spiritual goodness is described as the first stage of a lifelong journey from sin to redemption. Christians, for example, speak in terms of following a straight and narrow way; Buddhists attempt to walk the Eightfold Path, hewing to a set of injunctions laid down by Buddha himself.

The road to spiritual perfection can take many forms, depending on the beliefs and character of the traveler. As the images at left and on the following pages suggest, the journey may entail countless rituals of prayer and self-abasement, months or years of pilgrimage to holy places, physical ordeals to purify the soul, or even permanent retreat from the world of the flesh to the focused serenity of the monastic life.

The rewards at journey's end may vary, too. Members of Japan's Shugendo sect expect their purification rites to yield good fortune and quasi-magical powers in the here and now, whereas Christians and Muslims tend to equate spiritual perfection with personal salvation in a paradisiacal afterlife. And to the devout Buddhist, perfection—or enlightenment, in the language of Buddha's teachings—offers an escape from the relentless cycle of reincarnation into the deathless limbo called nirvana. Yet despite the diversity of their beliefs and methods, these seekers share a common goal—spiritual unity with the cosmos, a oneness with the creator.

In the time-exposure photograph above, Muslim pilgrims circle the cloth-draped Ka'ba, Islam's holiest shrine, as they prepare to leave Mecca after several days of worship. Completing at least one trip to Mecca is a religious duty for every devout Muslim. To manage it, some spend their life's savings on the airfare or ocean passage, while others take years to travel there on foot. Rigorous journeys are also enjoined on followers of Japan's Shugendo movement, a sect founded in the seventh century. Laden with heavy packs and forbidden to eat, Shugendo pilgrims like those at left are said to experience hell and redemption during their ritual mountain climbs—here, up 9,000-foot Mount Ontake. At its summit, each seeker confesses his faults and is hung by a rope over the mountain's edge as he contemplates whether to sin again.

101

In a spectacular display of ritual self-purification, Mayan village elders (below) walk over fiery coals during a Yucatán religious festival. At center, a Tibetan Buddhist lying prostrate before a shrine undergoes a more introspective rite; such devotions, which are meant to humble the worshiper, may last hours, days, or even weeks. Shugendo followers endure similar ordeals, including meditating for as long as half an hour under a near-freezing waterfall (far right). Although the devout remain quiet as the icy water pelts them, a European who learned the practice during sojourns in Japan likens the sensation to "someone driving a nail into your skull." Yet the faithful endure, perhaps driven by the tenet that one must "use the sword to open the mind to arrive at the harmonization of the individual and the universe."

Like the Tibetan Buddhist monks above, praying during a ritual said to eliminate barriers to enlightenment, many seekers of spiritual perfection gather in monastic groups to meditate or pray. Others, such as the Carthusian monk at right, find the company of fellow worshipers distracting. Living by strict rules established in the eleventh century, Carthusian monks sleep, eat, and work alone, meeting only for mass and—briefly—on Sundays and holy days. In their isolation, these contemplatives seek a personal relationship with the Divine, eventually coming to a mystical understanding of the world. Sickness and death are no longer frightening, and the annihilation of the ego is complete. "We give ourselves consciously to the will of God," explained one of the hermits. "We live here and in the afterlife at the same time."

CHAPTER 4

The Triumph of Good

eavy, swirling, wet snow choked the streets of Washington, D.C., on the afternoon of January 13, 1982, and offices closed early to let workers go home. Traffic on the Potomac River bridges to suburban Virginia was bumper to bumper. At nearby National Airport, Air Florida Flight 90 sat on the tarmac waiting to be cleared for takeoff. In a rear seat of the Boeing 737, Arland D. Williams, Jr., forty-six, a balding man with a neatly trimmed mustache and beard, stared out at the blizzard. A senior examiner with the Federal Reserve Bank of Atlanta, Williams had come to Washington on business. That job was now done, and in a few minutes he would be on his way to an assignment in sunny Tampa, Florida.

Scheduled takeoff time—2:15 p.m.—came and went. Passengers fidgeted and peered out at dimly visible snowplows and at mechanics spraying the wings of the plane with deicing fluid. Finally, the snow let up a bit, and at 3:37 p.m. the plane was cleared for takeoff. Flight 90 lined up behind fifteen other jetliners and about twenty minutes later roared down the runway. As it lifted into the gray sky shrouding the city, the plane shuddered, fighting to gain altitude. It barely cleared one railroad bridge and then another. Dead ahead was the 14th Street bridge, packed with the automobiles of commuters heading home. Then, just two minutes into its flight, the plane's engines seemed to stall. The crippled jet faltered, its belly raking the surface of the car-choked bridge; it broke in two and skidded into the frozen river. The fuselage, with its rows of passengers still buckled into their seats, tore through the ice and sank. The tail section stayed afloat, with five people—two men and three women—clinging to the torn metal. Another man struggled in the water a short distance away.

A United States Park Police helicopter soon roared over the crash site and hovered low over the survivors. Paramedic Eugene Windsor threw a lifeline to the man treading water about ten feet from the plane's tail and carried him to the Virginia shore a hundred yards away. The chopper returned and aimed the line at a bearded man who seemed unharmed and more alert than the others. Arland Williams caught the lifeline and without hesitation passed it on to flight attendant Kelly Duncan, who was the only crew member to survive. She was then safely lifted to shore.

The helicopter raced back, this time with two lifelines. Windsor aimed one at Williams, but once more the man passed it on. Again and again Williams deferred to the other survivors, until only he remained clinging to the plane's sinking debris. One last time the chopper came in low to throw a lifeline to Williams. But by this time Arland Williams was gone, his strength stolen by the icy black water that finally engulfed him.

According to friends and relatives, Williams was a happy man. A divorced father of two children, he was planning a second marriage. He seemed to have everything to live for. And yet, as the rescue helicopter's paramedic said afterward, "he put everyone else ahead of himself. Everyone."

Those who knew Arland Williams describe him as an ordinary man; according to his mother, he was "just average." Yet the kind of selfless sacrifice that Williams made on that blustery January afternoon is usually ascribed to heroes or saints, not to "average" individuals. The deeds of the Georgia bank examiner seem to demonstrate that ordinary men and women are capable of drawing on a powerful reserve of simple goodness.

Human beings are perpetually caught in tension between the desire to be good, to act in a moral, selfless way, and the temptation to be evil—or if not evil exactly, just selfish or unthinking. Many religions teach that to attain good-

ness, one must learn to accept divine love and to praise the god that is its source. Religious ascetics and mystics endure physical hardships that they believe will bring them closer to the source of good. Others work toward that end by serving humankind; Mother Teresa, who has devoted her life to nursing the poor of India, exemplifies good in this form. And stories abound of humble men, women, even children, who have experienced mysterious, miraculous phenomena thought to be sent from on high in return for acts of devotion or human kindness.

Not surprisingly, secular philosophers and scientists approach the question of goodness in a very different manner. According to social theorist Ernest Becker, human beings have always been amazed by their "inner yearning to be good, an inner sensitivity about the way things ought to be." This sensitivity, or conscience, which constitutes a moral law within each person, was a sublime mystery to eighteenth-century German philosopher Immanuel Kant. He felt there was no explanation for it, that it is just an intrinsic element of human nature.

Many scientists, too, believe goodness to be an innate human characteristic, even going so far as to suggest that human beings are genetically programmed to act altruistically. Charles Darwin was one of the first to investigate the biological roots of altruism in the animal kingdom. He found that, contrary to the basic evolutionary theory of the survival of the fittest, some creatures inten-

As spectators watch from bridge and riverbank, a rescue helicopter lifts survivors of a 1982 Air Florida crash out of the icy Potomac River. From such tragedies genuine altruists often emerge: With complete disregard for his own welfare, Georgia bank examiner Arland D. Williams, Jr. (inset), one of only six passengers who climbed out of the plane's wreckage alive, repeatedly refused the helicopter's lifeline until everyone else had been recovered from the 31 degree Fahrenheit water. By the time the rescue workers returned for him, Williams had disappeared beneath the river's surface.

tionally sacrifice themselves for others. According to the theory of kin selection, outlined in his 1859 work, *On the Origin of Species by Means of Natural Selection,* individual animals protect others of their species at great risk to themselves. Zebras, moose, and other grazing animals, for example, place themselves between their young and attackers. Soldier ants fight to the death to defend their colonies. And a vervet monkey warns its kin of approaching danger by vocalizing one of four different alarms—one each for flying, earthbound, and tree-climbing predators, and one just for snakes. The alerted band of vervet monkeys thus knows exactly where the threat is coming from and where to hide. But the sentinel, who attracts attention by calling out, is more likely than the others to be caught and killed.

In 1975, Harvard University zoologist Edward O. Wilson and others in the field updated Darwin's theory to include the findings of modern genetics. Writing about "the morality of the gene," Wilson explains the evolution of ethics by showing how altruism, cooperation, sharing, and other types of moral behavior evolved as ways to ensure survival of the genes carried first by close relatives and ultimately by the whole species.

Scientists are delving more and more deeply into the role of genetics in altruistic behavior. When mothers in studies pretended to be hurt or in pain, children as young as one year old exhibited signs of great concern, suggesting that empathy may be hereditary. At the Minnesota Center for Twin and Adoption Research, studies were conducted on sets of twins who were reared apart in differing circumstances. The conclusions were expected to demonstrate that human behavior is only about 10 percent genetically influenced. In fact, the results indicated that heredity accounts for approximately 50 percent of the dif-

ferences in personality traits in the population at large.

Although altruism was not among the particular traits measured in the Minnesota Center study, it was central to the research conducted in the early 1980s by J. Philippe Rushton, a University of Western Ontario psychologist. In testing 573 pairs of twins, Rushton reached much the same conclusion as his Minnesota colleagues—that there was about a 50 percent chance that altruistic personality traits could be inherited. This does not mean, however, that parents who teach their children to be kind and considerate are wasting their time; it simply suggests that some individuals are more predisposed than others toward helping people, even when there is no apparent benefit to themselves.

hile the argument for hereditary altruism is compelling, societal influences should not be ignored. The human mind has an unparalleled capacity for learning certain behaviors through culture and experience. We absorb values, emotions, and ideas from the society in which we live, and environment has been shown to have a profound influence on the development of the innate human potential for altruism.

Consider, for example, the Kung, a nomadic people living in Botswana in southern Africa. Formerly called Bushmen or Hottentots, they are small, sharp-featured foragers who live off the land. The Kung village is noisy with laughter, gossip, and storytelling. Men and women talk endlessly and often sing and dance; they remain cheerful even while performing the most tedious chores. When hunters drift away to search for food, the blind, sick, and crippled stay behind with those who choose not to leave the camp. No one says who must hunt or gather or how much work anyone must do. Food is ceremoniously divided and passed out to all—including those who did not help collect it. The villagers do disagree and occasionally scream and scold, but the worst sin among the Kung is stinginess.

Conversely, in Uganda, about 1,700 miles northeast, live the Ik, a people vastly different from the Kung. Behind a stockade fence enclosing the village, families live in huts, each one isolated from the others by its own smaller stock-

A Saint Who Died of Kindness

In the centuries since the Catholic church first bestowed the title of saint, precise criteria have been set for judging exceptional holiness. There are two types of saints: martyrs, who have followed Jesus Christ's example and died for the faith; and confessors, who have manifested certain virtues—such as faith, hope, and charity—to a heroic degree. All candidates must also have a number of miracles to their credit—one for a martyr and two for a confessor. Then, after rigorous investigation, judgment by a panel of theologians, and final approval by the pope, the martyr or confessor is formally canonized.

Recently, though, these standards were tested by an unqualified act of heroism. During World War II, Maximilian Kolbe, a devout Franciscan friar from Poland, was imprisoned at Auschwitz. There, in 1941, as a reprisal for an escape, guards chose ten men to die. When one of the condemned cried out, lamenting his wife and children, Kolbe stepped forward and offered his life for that of the prisoner.

For decades after, people suffering from deadly diseases prayed for Father Kolbe to intercede, and two miracles were attributed to him. In 1971, he was beatified—a step toward sainthood—as a confessor, because he had died for a person rather than for the faith. Fellow Franciscans and the Polish church campaigned to have him canonized as a martyr. Years of reviewing evidence for Kolbe's cause ensued, until, in 1982, against the advice of a panel he had convened to look into the matter, Pope John Paul II declared Father Kolbe a martyr. It was clear to many people that the Polish pontiff had unofficially created a new category—martyr for charity—when he quoted the Gospel of Saint John: "There is no greater love than this, that a man should lay down his life for his friends."

ade. The Ik fear and distrust relatives and neighbors as well as outsiders. Instead of sharing the food they find, they gobble it down in secret. For the Ik, it is a waste of food to give any to the sick or old; the few elderly in the community are emaciated. Although groups of Ik children start off to the mountains in the morning chattering gaily, they are not out on a romp—they must find their own provisions, for their parents put them out on their own by the age of four.

The simple societies of the Kung and the Ik are admittedly extreme examples of how cultures can foster or inhibit the growth of altruistic tendencies. Yet in the highly developed societies of today, people are also greatly affected by the actions and attitudes of those around them. A tragic event that occurred in 1964, in the New York City borough of Queens, brought this fact home to millions who saw or read the news accounts.

It happened on a cold March night at three a.m., in a working-class neighborhood. A young woman named Kitty Genovese had just parked her car a few blocks from her apartment building and was hurrying home, when she was suddenly grabbed by a strange man. In the eerie glow of a streetlamp, she was brutally stabbed.

She screamed, lights went on in the surrounding buildings, windows were thrown open, and someone shouted at the man. The attacker disappeared, yet no one came to the aid of the woman lying on the sidewalk. She struggled to her feet and staggered toward her apartment building. But before she could reach safety, the attacker reappeared and stabbed Genovese a second time. Screaming that she was dying, her strength ebbing away, the young woman slowly crawled to her doorway. Again, attention was aroused, but still no one came to help her. Then, unbelievably, the attacker appeared again, this time to finish the job in the building's entranceway. Only then—more than half an hour after the first attack—did someone call the police. When they arrived, Kitty Genovese was dead.

During their investigation, police discovered that thirty-eight people witnessed the young woman's murder yet did nothing until it was too late to save her. Some thought the confrontation was a lovers' quarrel, others chose not to get involved, still others were afraid. The story horrified the city and the nation. Kitty Genovese's death led many commentators to bemoan the impersonality, indifference, and alienation of modern urban life. But two young New York City psychologists, John Darley and Bibb Latané, were not convinced. "We suddenly had an insight," Latané recalls. "Maybe it was the very fact that there were thirty-eight people that accounted for their inactivity. Maybe each of the thirty-eight knew that a lot of other people were watching—and that was why they did nothing."

Through their subsequent experiments, Darley and Latané established what is now called the bystander effect, which maintains that the number of people present in an emergency situation determines the incidence of intervention by the witnesses. The psychologists developed three hypotheses to account for the bystander effect: Each witness is hesitant to act in front of the others until he or she knows what is called for; seeing others do nothing makes each witness think that inactivity is appropriate; each thinks the number of witnesses spreads the responsibility and lessens each individual's obligation to do something. The witnesses to the murder of Kitty Genovese, therefore, may not have been cold and uncaring; it is likely they were inhibited from action by a kind of tacit peer pressure.

The investigations of scientists and psychologists provide fascinating, if inconclusive, theories about the origin of goodness. But for thousands of years most people, when confronted with questions about what constitutes good and evil and how to make the right moral choices, have sought guidance from religion. Whether goodness is innate or not, religions have preached that by living a good life one can transcend the duality of good and evil and reach unity with the divine. Followers are encouraged to hew closely to moral codes that derive their authority from the deity. Those who stay the righteous course are usually promised the bliss of paradise, while those who transgress are threatened with the punishments of hell. The Hindu and Buddhist belief in reincarnation serves this moral purpose through the doctrine of karma (meaning "action" or "deed"), which teaches that people achieve a desirable rebirth as a result of good deeds in their previous lives.

A unique value of religion is found not in its moral codes, however, but in its mysticism. Mystics, saints, and yogis are generally not content merely to live good moral lives, although most are scrupulous about following the moral rules. Rather, they seek to experience the source of good—whatever they believe it to be—directly.

Historians trace the origins of religious mysticism to shamanism, perhaps the earliest ecstatic religion. According to Mircea Eliade, author of *Shamanism: Archaic Techniques of Ecstasy,* shamanism is integrally related to the paradise myth that is central to the mythologies of various cultures. "These myths refer to a time when communication between heaven and earth was possible; in consequence of a certain event or a ritual fault, the communication was broken off; but heroes and medicine men are nevertheless able to reestablish it," he wrote. By entering an ecstatic state, induced by ritual dancing and the invocation of spirits, the shaman is believed able to return to that time, visiting heaven and hell to talk with gods, spirits of the dead, and animals.

From these shamanic roots sprang a variety of techniques used by mystics the world over to induce ecstasy, detach themselves from the physical world, and become closer to their gods. Many of these practices involve extreme physical austerities. The Japanese *yamabushi,* or "mountain ascetics," for example, meditate under ice-cold waterfalls wearing only a loincloth or walk barefoot over hot coals. Some Hindu yogis look directly into the sun for long periods of time, and Buddhists may stare into a source

Eyes closed and arms outstretched, Islamic Sufis—or mystics—twirl and chant as part of a sacred ritual. The movements of these whirling dervishes, as they are called, symbolize creation: One hand receives the manifestation of the Divine, and the other transforms it into the earth. The whirling dance, which continues until the dervishes swoon in rapture, is thought to ready them for mystical experiences, such as telepathic communication or a vision of the future.

of light, at circles of earth-colored clay or at blue flowers, until a trance state is induced.

Meditation and prayer are also considered pathways to union with the Divine. Followers may repeat holy words or formulas again and again, either silently or aloud, to empty their minds of earthly matters. One Buddhist sect repeats Buddha's name anywhere from 50,000 to 500,000 times each day. Some Sufis, who are Islamic mystics, practice a spinning dance known as the whirling of the dervishes, which may be accompanied by the chanting of Allah's name. There are also many explicitly sexual roads to ecstasy in Taoism, Tantric Buddhism, and Hinduism. All three employ sexual union to symbolize the merging of the male and female principles into one mystical union.

As disparate as they may seem, all of these practices have one thing in common: They are meant to free the mystic from the preoccupation with self that is thought to prevent humans from attaining or realizing the source of all good. Therefore the mystic does his or her best to cleanse, purify, or illuminate the self, and when all illusion has been removed, the mystic arrives at the source of divinity.

Most mystical traditions include accounts of adepts who allegedly possess extraordinary powers. Some are said to levitate, others to be impervious to pain. Although most of these phenomena can be attributed to highly disciplined control over body and mind, powers displayed by some Christian mystics remain a puzzle, described by the faithful as miracles from God.

Miracles are defined as amazing and inexplicable events that are thought to result from a power beyond that of human beings; in the language of religion, they are considered divine interventions that demonstrate the power of good. Although they are not the sole province of religion, many of the best known and best documented events thought of as miracles—healing the sick, raising the dead, feeding the multitudes—occurred in the history of Christianity, particularly that of the Catholic church.

Throughout history, miracles have been taken as signs of divine approval of a saintly or holy nature, and as such seem to have manifested themselves in a variety of supernatural ways. Perhaps the most impressive account of this type of miracle is preserved in the writings of Saint Teresa of Ávila, a Spanish nun born in 1515. As a child, Teresa displayed no interest in religion, but with the encouragement of a nun and a pious uncle, she joined a Carmelite order at the age of twenty. A devout ascetic, Teresa eventually founded a reformed order of nuns and supervised a total of seventeen convents. By all reports an intelligent and capable woman, Teresa was also subject to intense ecstatic states during which she occasionally levitated. She was embarrassed by these paranormal displays and wrote in her autobiography, "It was a very sore distress to me. I was afraid it would occasion much talk." Teresa tried mightily to keep her gift a secret; when she felt a levitation coming on, she would ask everyone to leave the room.

On more than one occasion, however, she was apparently caught unawares. According to Teresa's writings, one day she was preparing to approach the altar of the convent chapel when she was suddenly lifted from the ground in full view of the other nuns. And in the testimony of Sister Anne, a witness during the investigation leading to Teresa's canonization—begun only thirteen years after her death—Teresa once was "raised about half a yard from the ground." The young woman moved close enough to put her hands under Teresa's feet, where she remained until the ecstasy ended and Teresa "suddenly sank down." Other witnesses saw Teresa desperately try to resist the powerful uplifting force. When she began to levitate after communion one day, Teresa grabbed at a grill in an attempt to steady herself. In another instance, the seemingly weightless nun was singing with a choir when she began to levitate. An observer said she clutched at the floor mats to keep from rising—

but ascended anyway with the mats held firmly in her hand.

During such levitations, Teresa would lose consciousness, then wake up in some confusion when she came down. "It seemed to me . . . as if a great force beneath my feet lifted me up," she wrote. "After the rapture was over, I have to say that my body seemed frequently to be buoyant, as if all weight had departed from it, so much so that now and then I scarcely knew that my feet touched the ground."

ome critics have discounted the stories of the saint's powers—Catholic priest Robert Smith devoted a 1965 book, *Comparative Miracles,* to debunking such claims. Teresa's levitations were witnessed only by others in the convent, Smith says, and the mystic's accounts may be suspect, because she was in an altered state of consciousness when the levitations occurred. But many who study her life and writings are convinced of Saint Teresa's integrity. As if she knew her gifts would be questioned, Teresa once wrote of a supposed visitation from an angel, describing an ecstatic pain "so sweet that I beg God to let whoever thinks I'm not telling the truth taste it."

If the levitations of Saint Teresa remain questionable, the apparent hoverings and, in some instances, actual flights of Saint Joseph of Copertino are fairly well accepted, reportedly having been witnessed on more than a hundred occasions. Perhaps the most compelling incident occurred during the holy man's sojourn at Assisi in 1645. At that time the Spanish ambassador to the papal court, the high admiral of Castile, was passing through town and visited Joseph in his cell at the monastery. After returning to the church, the admiral told his wife of the visit, whereupon she expressed an interest in meeting with the friar as well. Accordingly, the father guardian of the religious community asked Joseph to go to the church and talk to the woman, to which Joseph replied, "I will obey, but I do not know whether I shall be able to speak with her." True to his words, as soon as he entered the sanctuary and gazed upon a statue of the Virgin Mary, Joseph soared over the heads of those present, coming to rest at the foot of the statue. After paying homage to the Virgin, he let out a shrill cry and flew back again, straight to his cell, leaving in his wake the admiral, his wife, and their various attendants, all speechless.

This and other evidence of Joseph's ecstatic levitations were evaluated a century later during canonization hearings. Pope Benedict XIV personally studied all details of the case and later wrote that a "favourable conclusion" had been reached, citing that "eye-witnesses of unchallengeable integrity gave evidence of the famous upliftings from the ground and prolonged flights of the aforesaid Servant of God when rapt in ecstasy."

An even more familiar—and controversial—physical manifestation of ecstasy in the lore of Christian mystics is that of stigmata, wounds resembling those received by Christ before and during the Crucifixion. Stigmata were first mentioned in the Bible by Saint Paul, in the Book of Galatians, chapter six, verse seventeen. "From henceforth let no man trouble me," he said, "for I bear in my body the marks of the Lord Jesus." Until the 1200s, however, many churchgoers assumed Saint Paul was speaking figuratively.

According to most Church historians, the first ascetic to receive the stigmata was Saint Francis of Assisi, founder of the Franciscan order. The event allegedly took place in 1224, during a forty-day retreat to Mount Alvenia in the Apennines. Francis had been praying for guidance in how best to please God; while consulting the Gospels for the answer, three times he had come upon references to the Passion of Christ. Then, on September 14, while praying on a hillside, the mystic suddenly had a vision of Christ on the cross. As the vision retreated, wounds simulating those of the divine martyr opened on Francis's hands, feet, and side.

Although Francis mostly covered the wounds, those who saw them noted that the lesions never healed or became inflamed. More astounding perhaps were reports that actual protuberances resembling nailheads formed in the punctures on his hands and feet. According to Francis's friend and biographer, Thomas of Celano, they were "not the prints of the nails but the nails themselves formed out of his flesh." And in a thirteenth-century text, Saint Bonaventure, the Italian bishop and theologian who became head of

the Franciscan order in 1257, describes the so-called nails in Francis's feet as protruding so far as to "prevent the soles from being set down freely upon the ground."

The only other man since Saint Francis known to carry stigmata was Padre Pio da Pietrelcina of Foggia, near Italy's Adriatic coast. As the story goes, in 1918, while alone in the choir celebrating the Feast of the Stigmata of Saint Francis, the Capuchin friar let out a piercing cry. His brothers found Padre Pio unconscious, bleeding profusely from the five wounds. Regularly thereafter, during mass, he would fall into rapture and blood would issue from the lesions. Public adulation for the friar became so great that the villagers refused to confess to anyone but him, and the Vatican was forced to send an emissary to calm the devout of Foggia.

The next year, Capuchin superiors invited two physicians to examine Padre Pio's wounds. Their reports describe scars or scabs on the skin, not deep fissures, and dispute claims of hemorrhages. One doctor ventured that the lesions were not artificially produced but were probably attributable to unconscious suggestion. The Church's ambiguous conclusion was that the stigmata were not necessarily supernatural in origin.

Padre Pio became known for another seemingly supernatural feat as well—that of bilocation, or appearing in two places at once. Sometimes the friar's bilocations reportedly took the form of what psychical researchers call an out-of-body experience, in that his spiritual and physical presences were felt or seen by observers in two different locations at once. At other times, witnesses claim to have seen Padre Pio's double.

By all accounts, Padre Pio seems to have visited the sick without ever leaving his own church. He was reported to have been seen throughout Italy, and in Austria, Uruguay, and Milwaukee, Wisconsin. On one occasion, a sick woman in Borgomanero, in northwest Italy, entreated him to cure her, and he is said to have bilocated to her side. When she asked him to leave some token of his visit, Padre Pio placed his stigmatized hand on the edge of her bed, impressing on it five bloodstains, each in the shape of a cross.

Wielding the fiery arrow of divine love, an angel pierces the heart of Saint Teresa of Ávila in this seventeenth-century sculpture. The work depicts a vision experienced by the Carmelite nun that left her "utterly consumed by the great love of God." Like many other Christian mystics, Teresa believed the frequent ecstatic visions and levitations she experienced signaled a complete surrendering to God, opening the way to true goodness and charity.

The linen is still on display today in the town.

Although the Catholic church has never made an official pronounce-ment on the nature of such physical phenomena as levitation, bilocation, and stigmata, some scientists, physi-cians, and Church officials have con-ducted independent investigations. Two noted physicists—Dr. Richard Mattuck of the University of Copenhagen and Dr. Evan Harris Walker of Johns Hopkins Uni-versity in Baltimore—believe levitation may be rooted in what they call the "thermal noise" theory of psychokinesis. They sug-gest that an object, or a human being, can be made to move by itself or defy the laws of gravity if a force, such as the human mind, interferes with the random movement of the object's subatomic particles. Writing from a Catholic view-point in his book *La Levitation,* translated from the French in 1928, author Olivier Leroy argues that levitation by holy people is the result of a "divine hallucination." He contends that God permits the mystic—and any observers of the feat—to perceive that he or she has levitated.

In the case of stigmata, it became apparent during the seventeenth and eighteenth centuries that many of the af-flicted shared characteristics of a disorder that came to be known as hysteria. In his early-twentieth-century writings on the physical phenomena of mysticism, Father Herbert Thurston offered that "it cannot be disputed that the ecstasy of the mystic and the trance of the hysterical patient are very closely allied and cannot always be readily distin-guished." Alternatively, Thurston suggested that stigmata may also result from self-inflicted wounds, perhaps occur-ring while the ascetic is in a trance state, or from what

Thurston called a "crucifixion complex," wherein the devout becomes so obsessed with the image of the crucified Christ that he or she unconsciously causes small blood vessels under the skin to break and bleed.

No doubt many of these same arguments could be applied when examining other religious miracles reported throughout time—such wondrous events as the spontaneous appearance of holy images, for example; paintings and statues that have bled or wept tears; and miraculous healings or cures. But perhaps the events that would be hardest to explain with conventional theories would be the reported appearances of the Virgin Mary. Dating from about 1800, the Virgin has allegedly made hundreds of visits to earth, intervening in the affairs of humans by appearing to select mortals, usually in times of social turmoil.

A supposed visit by the Virgin Mary to a French town called Lourdes precipitated one of the longest running, most closely observed, and most talked about of supernatural events. It began on a cold February day in 1858, when three little girls of the village set out to gather firewood at a spot called Massabielle. To get there, the trio had to ford the shallow but frigid waters of a small millstream. One of the girls, Bernadette Soubirous, was asthmatic; she hung back, watching her energetic companions wade shoeless through the icy water. As Bernadette knelt down and tentatively began taking off her own shoes, she felt a sharp gust of wind that lashed her hair and body but did not ripple the canal's water or rustle the trees. Then Bernadette looked into a nearby grotto and glimpsed a bright light from which emerged a vision of a beautiful young girl. The image was dressed in white and holding a sparkling rosary.

The apparition said nothing but seemed to motion to Bernadette to come closer. The girl dropped to her knees and prayed; afterward, the vision disappeared. Gathering up her

Image in a Cloak of Flowers

Since the time of Christ, there have been many accounts of so-called divine images—physical imprints, usually of the Virgin Mary or Jesus Christ, that have miraculously appeared on walls, windows, floors, or on the clothing of God's most humble servants. Perhaps the best known of these—now famed throughout the world as the image of the Virgin of Guadalupe—was bestowed on a young man in 1531, atop a hill called Tepeyacac near present-day Mexico City.

There, on a December morning, a radiant, dark-skinned apparition of the Virgin Mary is said to have beckoned to Juan Diego, an Aztec Indian and devout Catholic. The Virgin, who called herself Santa María de Guadalupe, spoke to Juan in Nahuatl, his native tongue, and entreated him to ask the bishop of Mexico to build her a church on the hill. The bishop listened patiently to Juan's story but explained that he needed proof of the apparition's divine nature before he could grant such a wish. Diego went back to the hill and was amazed to find that the Virgin had miraculously caused a garden of flowers to bloom in the desert around Tepeyacac.

Juan gathered some of the blooms into his cloak and took them to the bishop. When Juan unfolded his wrap, however, the awe-struck men saw that the flowers on the cloak's fabric had been replaced by a likeness of the Virgin Mary herself—imaginatively represented here in this popular twentieth-century devotional painting. The bishop fell to his knees in reverence and begged Juan Diego's forgiveness. He vowed to erect a church in the Virgin's honor, and today the Basilica of Our Lady of Guadalupe displays the cloak, its holy image apparently unfaded after more than 400 years.

shoes, Bernadette crossed the canal—exclaiming that the water was now warm—and told her friends what had happened. She swore them to secrecy, but the two girls could not wait to tell all.

Again and again, Bernadette returned to Massabielle, now accompanied by numerous onlookers. She would kneel before the grotto, arms outstretched, her face pinched and colorless. Once, in the throes of ecstasy, the girl heard the apparition say, "Drink and wash at the spring and eat of the grass that you find there." Bernadette fell to her knees and began scratching at the ground. A little water seeped up, and the girl put it to her lips. By early afternoon that day, passersby noticed a trickle of water flowing from the spot where Bernadette had gouged the earth; by evening a spring had appeared and a pool had begun to form.

A few days later, the apparition appeared again, demanding that Bernadette "tell the priests to build a chapel here." The girl dutifully carried the message to the parish priest, who in turn demanded, "If it is really Our Lady, let her work a miracle." Soon after, a blind quarryman rubbed his eyes with water from the spring and instantly regained his sight, a fact confirmed by the man's doctor.

An analysis of the spring water revealed nothing out of the ordinary. Yet since that day, thousands claim to have been healed in the waters at Lourdes, and millions more—many close to death—flock every year to the churches built there to honor the Blessed Mother.

The Virgin is said to have made an equally dramatic appearance to three peasant children in the town of Fátima, Portugal, during World War I. On a spring day in 1916, nine-year-old Lucia dos Santos, eight-year-old Francisco Marto, and his six-year-old sister, Jacinta, were tending sheep in a hollow just outside the town. According to the youngsters, an apparition of a boy suddenly materialized and instructed them to pray. Twice more that year the angel appeared to them. Then, on May 13, 1917, the three children were again in the hollow and had just knelt in prayer, when a flash of lightning pierced the cloudless sky. As they ran down the slope to escape the coming rain, there appeared before

them a dazzling young woman who wore a white veil bordered with gold. She told the children that she was from heaven and that she wished them to return to the hollow on the thirteenth day of each month for the next five months.

The three agreed not to discuss their adventure with anyone, but little Jacinta could not keep quiet. She told her parents that she had seen the Virgin Mary, even though the apparition had not identified herself as such. News of the visitation spread like a firestorm, and inevitably some villagers accused the children of making up the fantastic story. Yet, the apparition had promised to return on June 13, and at about midday the children went to the hollow, accompanied by some fifty residents of Fátima.

oon Lucia pointed to the sky and the three children claimed to see the Virgin gliding down to them from the heavens. The other spectators saw nothing, although during the event the bright sunlight supposedly dimmed and they claimed to hear the sound of indistinct whisperings. According to the youngsters, the apparition then disclosed the first of several secrets to Lucia.

When the three children returned to the hollow the following month, a crowd of 5,000 awaited them. Reportedly, the apparition again spoke to Lucia and urged the girl to pray every day for the end of the war. Lucia, in turn, asked for a miracle so that the onlookers would be convinced of the Virgin's authenticity. The apparition agreed and set October 13 as the date. This incident touched off a wave of religious sentiment throughout Portugal that greatly upset the country's anticlerical government. An investigation was launched, and the children were detained and strongly urged—apparently under the threat of being boiled in oil—to say they had been lying. The youngsters refused but missed the Virgin's promised August 13 visit.

The next month saw 30,000 pilgrims in the hollow near Fátima. The children arrived, and according to onlookers, the sun once again began to dim; stars could be seen in the noontime sky, and an orb of white light appeared. Suddenly the hollow was showered with a rain of white flower petals, which mysteriously disappeared before reaching the ground. The apparition, meanwhile, had appeared to Lucia and told her that more prayer was needed to end the war and again promised a miracle on the next visit—October 13.

The following month, the government sent troops to Fátima in case the crowd, which had now reached 70,000, became unruly. The apparition reportedly appeared once more and proclaimed that the war would soon end. Then, the clouds parted and a huge silver disk—which some observers believed was the sun—began floating in the sky. The disk began to whirl, turning on itself and throwing off colored flames in all directions. One newspaper reporter described the disk as making "sudden incredible movements outside all cosmic laws." The spectacle lasted about ten minutes and ended with the disk diving through the sky. The heat caused by its descent panicked the crowd, but then the orb suddenly stopped and soared off again. This alleged miracle, dubbed by scholars "the dance of the sun," was apparently witnessed by all 70,000 onlookers. It was the last time the apparition appeared in the hollow at Fátima.

In 1941, at the request of her bishop, Lucia wrote out a description of her supposed conversations with the Virgin Mary. It was then that the girl revealed some of the secrets she claimed were entrusted to her. The first was a vision of hell, which had terrified her; the second was the message that another world war might destroy the earth if humankind did not stop offending God. Lucia could not bring herself to reveal the last of the secrets to anyone but Pope Pius XII, although it has been rumored to

include the prophecy of a third, and final, global conflict.

Such visions of the Virgin Mary as occurred in Fátima and Lourdes often display similar characteristics, according to Nicholas Perry and Loreto Echeverría, authors of *Under the Heel of Mary,* a 1988 book examining the phenomenon. Among the similarities, the apparition appeared as a three-dimensional figure, presented to its child-seers glimpses of heaven and hell, and entrusted these witnesses with secrets. These characteristics were echoed as well in possibly

Pilgrims seeking miraculous cures in the French town of Lourdes pay homage to the Virgin Mary at church services—here broadcast to an overflow crowd in a meadow—and immerse themselves in tubs of water believed to have healing powers. The Virgin supposedly revealed a curative spring to a devout local girl in 1858. Since then, thousands who have "taken the waters" have claimed recovery from various illnesses.

the most recent alleged sightings of the Blessed Mother, which began in 1981 in Medjugorje, a remote region of Yugoslavia. There, as in Fátima, the sightings were witnessed by a number of young people, ranging in age from ten to eighteen, on a hill outside the village. And once again, the Virgin promised to impart secrets to the seers, one of which—the exact date of Mary's birth—is to be made public only with the pope's permission.

Supernatural phenomena have also been reported in Medjugorje. Many claimed to have seen hosts of angels, and in 1982, on the Feast of the Sacred Heart, eyewitnesses reported "stars rotating in the sky." Soon tens of thousands of pilgrims converged on the village, provoking a swift reaction from the country's Communist rulers. Police questioned the young visionaries, arrested several priests, and even strip-searched nuns in an effort to uncover a hoax.

Yet the seers remain undaunted, and according to them, the apparition continues to appear, now in the safety of a small room in the parish rectory. They gather often to listen closely to the Virgin's secret whisperings, for—according to their story—she has told them these will be her last appearances in our time.

Some who claim to have conversed with the Virgin Mary report that her coming was heralded by the appearance of an angel. Angels are typically thought to be attendants and messengers of a supreme deity, and the concept that they help humankind achieve a proper rapport with a god is universal in folklore, legend, and theology.

The ancients believed not only in spirits that stood between the gods and humans but in beings that warded off evil as well. The ancient Egyptians, Mesopotamians, Hittites, and Persians all believed in winged creatures—some having the bodies of animals with human heads—who were charged with vanquishing demons. Some cultures ascribed guardianship rights to these spirits. The Egyptians thought that every living person had an otherworldly double, or ka, that was born with him and protected him throughout life. And the dualistic Persians believed that every human was attended by heavenly twins: a good and an evil spirit.

The Persian gods were unseated when the prophet Zoroaster—believed to have lived in the sixth century BC—declared that Ahura Mazda, or Ohrmazd, was the one and only God. Zoroaster knew that his people had been honoring familiar gods for centuries, however, so he recast some of them as "bounteous immortals," or angels; the rest he condemned as demons. And Mani, the Babylonian prince who founded the dualistic religion of Manicheanism, was often inspired, it is said, by an angel called at-Taum, or twin. This angel supposedly guided the prophet throughout his life and attended him at his death.

Angels occur in other Asian and Middle Eastern beliefs as well. Although Taoism gives no official place to angels as such, spirits that bestow blessings and cast out demons appear in Chinese and Japanese religions. Under Buddhism, the bodhisattvas—the holy Buddhas-to-be—resemble angels in that they are said to guide humankind toward enlightenment. And the angels of Islam, called *malaika,* or messengers, are the guardians of humanity, writing down everything people do. They report their findings to Muhammad, Islam's prophet, and are entrusted with blessings to bring to earth.

The pervasiveness of celestial beings in the sacred teachings of Islam and Judeo-Christianity led in the Middle Ages to a system of ranking angels and giving them specific functions and dominions. Angels were reported to govern the four points on the compass and the four elements of earth, air, water, and fire. They were credited with moving the stars and tending plants, and they supposedly graced the birth of each child. Every day of the week, each season, and each hour was said to have a protecting angel.

The guardian angels that reportedly appear to humans in times of need or to deliver divine messages are said to take on many different guises. They may come as visions or dreams, it is believed, or as clouds, a light in the sky, or even disguised as humans. In her 1975 book, *Appointment in Jerusalem,* author Lydia Prince describes an encounter in 1929 with what she believed to be an angel. Prince was

Believers gather on a hilltop near Medjugorje in central Yugoslavia, where, in 1981, five children said they beheld the Virgin Mary. Many pilgrims who have since made the arduous climb claimed to see an apparition of Mary as a swirling sun or to hear her speak. Some scholars interpret these strange phenomena as "comforting illusions" imagined by those in spiritual or physical anguish.

caught in a conflict between warring Arabs and Jews; bullets were flying in the streets, and she was alone, caring for a small child, in a house whose water supply had been cut off. To stay inside promised a slow death from thirst; to go outside carried the certainty of being shot.

Quietly asking God's help, Prince gathered up the child and stepped into the street. It was eerily quiet. She negotiated barricades set up by the street guerrillas but soon came to one she could not scale while holding the child. As she despaired of what to do, a tall young man dressed in European clothes suddenly appeared before her. Without a word spoken, he took the child, climbed over the barricade, and led Prince to the house of an Englishwoman she knew. She greeted her astonished friend, then looked around to thank the samaritan who had saved her. He had vanished.

When Prince looked back on her good fortune—the sudden quiet after nearly ceaseless gunfire, the arrival of unexpected help, the shelter of a friend's house—she concluded that the man was a guardian angel sent to save her and the child. Author Sophy Burnham describes a similar encounter in her 1990 work, *A Book of Angels.* Burnham and her husband were on a ski trip in France in 1964, when she took a nasty spill. She was sliding straight toward a sheer drop-off, she recalled, when a man dressed in black with luminous eyes skied toward her at great speed. He positioned himself between her and the cliff's edge, and Burnham slid into his legs. "It didn't hurt," she wrote. "Neither did he fall with the impact or even stumble and have to catch his weight." She thanked the stranger for saving her life; he made no answer but just skied off, never to be seen again.

According to a friend of Burnham's, an investment banker named Jack Moorman, guardian angels appear disguised as women as well as men. At the age of eight, Moorman recalled, he had been left alone at home one day. He was busy with a set of woodworking tools when a knife slipped and cut his finger to the bone. The boy was frightened and in pain; there was blood everywhere. Then the doorbell rang. Young Jack wrapped his hand in a towel and ran to answer the door, where he found a nurse in a white uniform asking for his parents. She came inside, cleaned and bandaged his wound, then left. He never found out who she was or why she had come. And she never returned. As a boy, Jack Moorman never questioned the nurse's timely appearance. But four decades later he admits how strange the encounter was and believes the nurse may have been an angel come to minister to him.

This angel from the Islamic tradition, created for an Imperial Turkish album, bears a cup and a flask as part of its many duties as a deceased mortal's guide to the afterlife. Also functioning as messengers of gods or as guardians of a person's earthly fate, angels are believed to steer humankind toward the realization of a greater and more perfect good.

Karen Hill's daughter, on the other hand, recognized her rescuers immediately. The family was picnicking in the Colorado mountains, Hill told Burnham, and her two children—a five-year-old daughter and a son two years older—were playing on the banks of a small stream. Suddenly the Hills heard their son scream: "We turned to see our daughter being sucked into the culvert. She had fallen on her head into the water. She was facedown holding on to the sides when my husband grabbed her out."

On the way home, Hill recalled, "I was holding her and telling her how proud I was that she held on and how strong she was. Then I gave her a small lecture on danger—to never give up, and so on. She looked at me and said, 'But Mommy, there were three tiny angels helping me; they told me to hold on, and I felt so strong.' "

According to angel lore, these heavenly helpers not only protect and guide their charges during earthly life, they also shepherd them to the afterlife—that mystical place in which everything good resides. There the righteous can spend eternity surrounded by unending earthly delights while enjoying freedom from earthly woes.

Not surprisingly, the heavens of different peoples tend to reflect their varying conceptions of pleasures. Valhalla, the heaven of the early Norsemen, was a place where warriors feasted and drank mead, went out to fight every day, and were miraculously cured of their battle wounds to fight

Shown here with a few of her orphaned charges in Calcutta, Albanian-born Mother Teresa lives and works according to a simple philosophy: To know God, the ultimate source of good, is to serve him. "It is Christ," says the Nobel Peace Prize winner, "whom you are touching in the poor."

again on the morrow. In Celtic myth, the Island of Avalon was a warm place without sorrow or death, and the Elysian Fields of the Greeks were located in blessed isles of abundance.

In the Pure Land of the Buddhists, human beings can rest contentedly; in the Garden of Eden, the blessed may regain innocence and come to know the Lord. Similarly, in Islamic tradition, heaven is the place where the Divine reigns, so the final happiness is the beatific vision of the supreme God, the source of all good.

Most living mortals can only imagine paradise; Emanuel Swedenborg claimed to have actually visited it. "Today's churchman knows almost nothing about heaven, hell, or his own life after death," the Swedish philosopher and visionary wrote in 1758. "To prevent so negative an attitude it has been made possible for me to be right with angels and talk to them person to person. I have also been allowed to see what heaven is like."

In Swedenborg's vision, the afterlife has five components: a spirit world where souls go immediately upon death, hell, and three heavens—a natural heaven, a spiritual heaven, and a celestial heaven. In the spirit world, as in life, it is up to the individual to choose good or evil, Swedenborg relates. Because faults and errors are more visible in this realm than on earth, however, souls can be educated to perfect their psychological and spiritual understanding. When they progress in wisdom and in love, they are transformed into angels and move on to one of the heavenly levels.

The angels populating Swedenborg's heavens live in communities, which are similar to but exceed those on earth, because they reflect the state of mind of the angels. There are parks and gardens and cities with avenues, streets, and squares. Members of the celestial choir live in houses "like the dwellings on earth which we call homes, except that they are more beautiful."

Angels of the so-called natural heaven busy themselves teaching the new arrivals in the spirit world. In the spiritual heaven, angels exercise their love through charity. They worship in stone churches and make and administer laws. The angels in the highest, or celestial, heaven, however, live in a state of primitive simplicity and childlike innocence, in harmony with nature. These angels are naked, says Swedenborg, "because nakedness corresponds to innocence." There are no elaborate churches, only wooden ones, and there are no clergy—the angels preach to one another.

But Emanuel Swedenborg's highest heaven is not simply a refuge of childlike delight. The angels are not without egotism or pride, he explains, and they suffer accordingly. Yet these character flaws are necessary, so that in overcoming them, the angels can develop their spiritual strength. Observes Swedenborg, the "perception and awareness of what is good is made more delicate by fluctuations between things pleasant and unpleasant."

Many theologians maintain that a belief in a transcendental realm of gods, miracles, and angels is necessary to provide a basis for good behavior and moral conduct. Others, however, point out that some people who do not subscribe to a belief in any religion or even in a god are no less moral than their devout brethren.

According to University of Buffalo professor Paul Kurtz, "If we remove the threat or fear of divine retribution, people will not necessarily rob, rape, and kill. If religious foundations are removed, morality does not collapse; nor does hedonic self-interest become the rule of the day." Kurtz is a leader of the secular humanist movement, a school of philosophy that contends that reason and science can explain human nature and that rejects any attempt to interpret the world in supernatural terms.

Secular humanists argue that only by discounting a divine order can people begin to recognize that every individual is responsible for his or her own actions. They believe that transcendentally based ethics exist at a lower stage of moral evolution, because they exalt obedience to commandments and inflexible rules rather than individual choice. The ethics of humanism seek to develop individuals capable of ethical deliberation. The humanist position is exemplified in the Unitarian church and in the views of many earlier philosophers, going back to the ancient Greeks.

In contrast, ethical objectivists, or absolutists, hold that moral values have a reality of their own—that what is good is independent of what any particular person thinks or likes. One of the greatest proponents of this viewpoint was Plato, who thought that good was an eternal and unchanging principle or idea that stood apart and transcendent. The problem is that even if such ideals as justice, truth, virtue, and good do exist, Platonic theory does not offer any practical way to use them in solving moral quandaries. However, the writings of eighteenth-century German philosopher Immanuel Kant offer some specific guidelines. His "categorical imperative" dictates that people "act only on that maxim whereby thou canst at the same time will that it should become a universal law." Kant derived this moral tenet from a complex chain of reasoning, but it could be seen as a restatement of the golden rule: Do unto others as you would have them do unto you.

Citing his talks with God and angels, mystic Emanuel Swedenborg wrote in the 1700s that "Heaven is doing good from good-will; hell is doing evil from ill-will."

Out of Kant's categorical imperative came his well-known test of the validity of an ethical principle: Before initiating an action, a person must determine whether the maxim governing the act could become a universal rule for all humankind. Using this as a measure, then, it would not be ethical to cheat, lie, steal, or kill, because if these acts became universally accepted, moral conduct—or any normal life—would be impossible.

But in the eyes of those called subjectivists, all values are relative to each individual or group. Thus, the answer to the question "What is good?" depends on the determination of whether it promotes happiness. As espoused by Jeremy Bentham, the British philosopher who lived from 1748 to 1832, the basic idea is that good is that which produces "the greatest happiness of the greatest number" of people.

Subjectivism has also led to the modern concept of situation ethics, which many people find troubling. The concept suggests that few moral rules are truly universal. Thus, the Sixth Commandment, "thou shalt not kill," might seem to be all inclusive until one considers that soldiers are ordered to kill in war and honored for doing so. Capital punishment, euthanasia, and self-defense are also possible exceptions to the rule. The argument of subjectivists in such a case is that what is good or right depends on the situation.

One of the most uncomfortable problems posed in discussing situation ethics is the so-called lifeboat dilemma. In a hypothetical situation, a ship sinks in heavy seas and some survivors reach a lifeboat. Unfortunately, there are more people aboard than the boat can safely carry and every wave threatens to swamp the vessel. Obviously, unless the load is lightened, the boat will sink and all will drown. The moral question becomes, What is the right thing to do? One might ask for volunteers to go overboard and hope that altruists would sacrifice themselves. The survivors might draw straws to see who stays and who goes, or the strong might push the weak into the sea.

Similar dilemmas present themselves whenever people face the question of survival. But whether one's reaction to such a situation finds its root in ethics, religion, or the theory of genetically based altruism, it is often the case that such a human being as Arland Williams, the hero of the Air Florida flight, will commit a completely selfless act—without anticipation of reward of any kind and often at grave peril to oneself.

The hero is the stuff of myth in cultures all over the world. The fact is that everyday altruism is much more common than anyone imagines. Each year about nine million people give blood for the benefit of people they will never meet. Nearly half of all adults in the United States perform unpaid volunteer work for the betterment of others. And seven out of ten households contribute to charities without regard to the benefits of tax deductions. More dramatically, there are those like Swedish diplomat Raoul Wallenberg, who, when confronted with evil in its most heinous form, almost single-handedly saved thousands of Hungarian Jews from certain death at the hands of the Nazis in World War II. And an estimated 50,000 other nameless men and women risked their lives to rescue some 200,000 Jews from the horrors of the Holocaust.

If this heroic behavior is mysterious, it is also natural. In the mystical sphere, one's unity with the ultimate good results in ecstasy, sainthood, or enlightenment; in the moral and ethical arena, it results in love and compassion. By transcending the mistaken notion that humans are isolated and limited, the mystic and the ordinary good man and woman are brought to the same conclusion: that people are not disconnected individuals but are related to one another, part of a single unity.

It seems to be a characteristic of cosmic duality that all things are balanced in the end. What are two distinct and opposing entities unite to become a complete and balanced whole. But what seems like contradiction may in fact be paradox. "Were one asked to characterize the life of religion in the broadest and most general terms possible," wrote American psychologist and philosopher William James, "one might say that it consists of the belief that there is an unseen order, and that our supreme good lies in harmoniously adjusting ourselves thereto."

Hark! Heaven's Winged Host

Every visible thing in this world," declared Saint Augustine, a theologian who lived from AD 354 to 430, "is put under the charge of an angel." Indeed, although many people deem their very existence patently impossible, angels have been seen as the link between the supreme God and humankind throughout history and in almost every religion. They have acted as guardians and messengers and served as advisers, matchmakers, and even gravediggers. Yet their exact nature remains elusive.

"Angels are powers which transcend the logic of our existence," observes modern-day minister and author Walter Nigg. Nevertheless, countless scholars have sought to understand them in human terms. A sixth-century monk, for example, devised a heavenly hierarchy, revealing the names, ranks, and duties of various angels. And a group of fourteenth-century cabalists toiled at length to calculate the exact number of angels, finally arriving at a mind-numbing 301,655,722. More recently, a respected nature writer derived a formula for determining an angel's wingspan. His calculations, which assumed a weight of roughly 154 pounds, probably failed to account for one particularly outsize member of the celestial choir, said to have stood ninety-six miles high.

Such efforts notwithstanding, it is unlikely that the hard reality of science will ever truly reconcile with the dreamlike realm of angels, where the heavenly host—represented on the following pages in art drawn from the Christian tradition—is said to watch over the actions of all humankind.

A Guide to the Celestial Hierarchy

During the Middle Ages, scholars passionately argued such weighty questions as what angels look like and whether they have form or substance. Although their ideas generated lively debate, they yielded few answers.

Soon, however, there emerged a source book on angels that was embraced by such Catholic luminaries as Pope Gregory the Great and Albertus Magnus. Thought to have been written in the sixth century by a Syrian monk called Dionysius, *The Celestial Hierarchy* divided angels into nine ranks, or choirs. These ranks, identified by name, position, and function, were then organized into three ascending levels of importance *(right)*. This heavenly pecking order mirrored the organization of the Church and was quickly accepted.

Although in time challenges did arise, the idea of an angelic hierarchy continued to fire the imaginations of poets, mystics, and scholars. The structure influenced Dante's *Divine Comedy* as well as John Milton's *Paradise Lost* and figured in the visions of twelfth-century seer and abbess Hildegard von Bingen. And even thirteenth-century theologian Saint Thomas Aquinas found inspiration in Dionysius's orderly view of the cosmos. In 1259, Aquinas drew large crowds at the University of Paris with a week-long seminar on angels. His lectures formed the foundation of angel lore and immortalized Saint Thomas as "the Angelic Doctor."

This wheel of angels, revealed in a vision to the twelfth-century mystic Hildegard von Bingen, includes the nine ranks set out by the monk Dionysius. The angels form a series of concentric circles, with those choirs of greatest importance closest to the hub, the source of all creation.

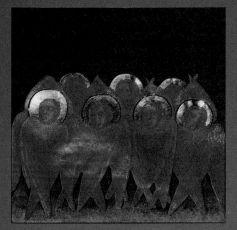

Seraphim, the highest ranking of Diony-sius's nine choirs of angels, are said to be creatures of light and fire. Possessing three pairs of flame-red wings, they are believed to incite mortals toward divine love.

Cherubim, meaning "fullness of knowl-edge," are considered to be the keepers of celestial records and the bestowers of wis-dom. Their ranks were said to include Satan before his fall from grace.

Often referred to as "the bearers of God," thrones are sometimes pictured as a ha-loed head above a fiery wheel. Their sup-posed duty is to contemplate divine justice.

Dominions, who manifest the majesty of God, are believed to regulate the duties of all the other angels. Members of this choir are commonly pictured holding an orb or scepter as a symbol of their authority.

Virtues, who serve as bestowers of grace and valor, are said to carry out the per-formance of divine miracles. In addition, they guide the movements of the planets.

Angels called powers are thought to im-pose order on the workings of the universe and toil to keep the forces of evil at bay.

Principalities are reputedly engaged in the welfare of human states and nations, and they sometimes appear to instruct the leaders of the human world. They are also regarded as the guardians of religion.

Archangels supposedly concern themselves with affairs that affect multitudes of peo-ple, particularly in matters of belief. As messengers, these celestial beings are gen-erally associated with grave tidings.

On the lowliest rung of the celestial ladder are angels, considered the guardians of the human race. Every physical object on earth, it is said, is entrusted to their care.

Gabriel, who slew the gargantuan offspring of the celestial rebels, is sometimes referred to as the angel of revelation. According to legend, he will sound the final call at doomsday.

God's All-Knowing Nobles

Of all the choirs of angels, archangels are believed to have the most profound effect on humankind. They are said to bring important tidings from the Almighty to earth and, as recounted in the Dead Sea Scrolls, once saved the human race from rebel angels who were setting the world to ruin.

In this tale, perhaps the strangest and most dramatic in angel lore, 200 angels known as "the Watchers" once descended from heaven to sample the pleasures of earth. In time, each of the 200 took an earthly spouse. These unions produced children of extraordinary size, who quickly devoured the world's food. To satisfy their enormous appetites, the angel-children roamed the earth slaughtering every species of bird, beast, reptile, and fish. Finally, the ravenous creatures turned on one another, stripping flesh from the bones of their fellows and slaking their thirst in rivers of blood.

As this wave of destruction washed over the earth, the anguished cries of humankind reached four powerful archangels—Uriel, Raphael, Gabriel, and Michael—who upon orders from God enacted a swift retribution. First, Uriel descended to earth to warn Noah of a coming deluge, advising him to prepare an ark to carry his family and a menagerie of creatures to safety. Raphael then fell upon the leader of the Watchers, bound him hand and foot, and thrust him into eternal darkness. Next, Gabriel, charged with slaying the dissenters' offspring, encouraged the monstrous angel-children to fight one another. Finally, Michael trussed up the remaining Watchers, forced them to witness the deaths of their progeny, and condemned them to eternal torment. Only then did the heavens open up and wash away the last traces of the destruction that the fallen angels had wrought.

Shown here vanquishing an evil demon, the warlike Michael is said to have forced the rebel Watchers to bear witness to the havoc they created. Considered the greatest of all angels, Michael is responsible for weighing souls for final reckoning.

Variously depicted in roles of guardian and muse, angels are said to dispense both

Unseen Angels Who Protect and Inspire

"Good day to you and your companion," runs a once-common French greeting. The phrase was used even for solitary travelers, because everyone was thought to have a guardian angel.

Mountain climber Francis Sydney Smythe believed he had an invisible guide during a solo trek up Mount Everest in 1933. He recalled sensing a powerful but friendly presence: "In its company I could not feel lonely, neither could I come to any harm."

Although Smythe was not certain he

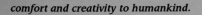

comfort and creativity to humankind.

was shadowed by a guardian angel, he treated it with courtesy. "As I halted and extracted some mint cake from my pocket," he reminisced, "it was so near and so strong that instinctively I divided the mint into two halves and turned around with one half in my hand to offer it to my 'companion.' "

Guardian angels are also said to inspire their charges. The seventh-century English poet Caedmon claimed he was mute until an angel bid him sing; the poet responded by writing sacred verse. And English artist and mystic William Blake revealed that, as a boy, he saw angels in the trees; thereafter, he was compelled to honor them in his paintings and his poetry.

Calling for the Heavenly Messengers

Throughout history, angels are said to have revealed themselves to humans to deliver messages or instructions and to help those in need. But many people believe that rather than waiting for an angel to appear, it is possible to summon humankind's helpers to earth.

For Native Americans, the ritual beckoning of one's guardian spirit could be life's most important experience. To invoke the spirit, a brave would go naked into the wilderness to fast and endure other hardships. The ordeal would produce otherworldly visions, culminating in the appearance of a protective force that would accompany the brave throughout his life.

Over time, less traditional methods of summoning an angel have included magical incantations and potions. Some occultists have counseled that a simple change of wardrobe can help: Soft-green clothing may hail a guardian angel; garments of sapphire blue might draw a healing spirit. Others have suggested that meditating on angel lore might leave one more receptive to heavenly visitations. In time, these theorists speculate, a heightened sensitivity—what one adherent terms "angel consciousness"—may make it possible to call upon angels at will.

A turn-of-the-century German poet, Christian Morgenstern, held a similar view. "All secrets (angels included) lie before us in perfect openness," he wrote. "There are no mysteries as such, only uninitiated of all degrees."

ACKNOWLEDGMENTS

The editors thank these individuals and institutions for their valuable assistance in the preparation of this volume: Professor Roger D. Abrahams, Department of Folklore and Folklife, University of Pennsylvania, Philadelphia; François Avril, Conservateur, Département des Manuscrits, Bibliothèque Nationale, Paris; Brother Robert, Abtei Mariawald, Heimbach, Germany; Sergio Campagnolo, Padua, Italy; Germano Donati, Narni, Italy; Jane Gallop, Department of English, University of Wisconsin, Milwaukee; Ara Güler, Istanbul; Father Peter Gumpel, S.J., Rome; Claus Hansmann, Munich; Instituto Archeologico Germanico, Rome; Heidi Klein, Bildarchiv Preussischer Kulturbesitz, Berlin; James R. Lewis, Director of the Santa Barbara Center for Humanistic Studies, Santa Barbara, California; Hilmar Pabel, Rimsting, Germany; Bruna Polimeni, Rome; Philip Rawson, Dorchester, Dorset, England; Liselotte Renner, Bayerische Staatsbibliothek, Handshriftenabteilung, Munich; Pater Andreas Rohring, Mariannhill Kloster, Würzburg, Germany; Father Dietmar Seubert, Rome; Simonetta Toraldo, Rome; Abbie Ziffren, Department of Religion, George Washington University, Washington, D.C.

PICTURE CREDITS

Credits for illustrations from left to right are separated by semicolons, from top to bottom by dashes.

Cover: Art by Rob Wood of Stansbury, Ronsaville and Wood, Inc. 6, 7: Wim Swaan/Camera Press, London; Manfred Grohe, Kirchentellinsfurt. 8, 9: J. L. Nou, Explorer, Paris; Werner Forman Archive, London (Haiphong Museum). 10: From *Tantra: The Indian Cult of Ecstasy*, by Philip Rawson, Thames and Hudson, London, 1973. 11: Jean-Loup Charmet, Paris; Roderick Hook, courtesy the Wheelwright Museum of the American Indian, No. P4#4A. 12: Hirmer Fotoarchiv, Munich—Gianni Dagli Orti, Paris—Foto Claus Hansmann, Munich. 13: Sven Gahlin Collection, London. 14: Foto Claus Hansmann, Munich—courtesy the Trustees of the British Museum, London. 15: Bildarchiv Preussischer Kulturbesitz, Berlin; Rijksmuseum Amsterdam, Netherlands. 17: Scala, Florence. 19: Gemeentemuseum Den Haag, courtesy Cordon Art—© 1990 M. C. Escher Heirs/Cordon Art, Baarn, Holland. 20-22: © 1990 M. C. Escher Heirs/Cordon Art, Baarn, Holland. 25: The Charles Walker Collection/Images Colour Library, London. 27: Courtesy the Trustees of the British Museum, London. 28: From *The Atlas of Mysterious Places*, edited by Jennifer Westwood, Weidenfeld & Nicholson, New York, 1987. 29: Jean-Loup Charmet, Paris. 30: Foto Claus Hansmann, Munich. 32, 33: Werner Forman Archive, London. 34: Bildarchiv Preussischer Kulturbesitz, Berlin. 35: Foto Claus Hansmann, Munich. 36, 37: From *Alchemy: The Ancient Science*, by Neil Powell, Doubleday, Garden City, N.Y., 1976; Ann Ronan Picture Library, Taunton, England—Bayerische Staatsbibliothek, Munich. 39: Jean-Loup Charmet, Paris. 41-47: Art by John Collier. 49: Ara Güler, Istanbul. 50: The Augustus C. Long Health Sciences Library, Columbia University, New York. 51: Gerd Ludwig/Woodfin Camp & Associates, Inc. 52, 53: American Museum of Natural History; art by Rob Wood of Stansbury, Ronsaville and Wood, Inc., from *TimeFrame: The Age of God-Kings* © 1987 Time-Life Books Inc. 54: Sören Hallgren/Statens Historika Museum, Frey, Sweden. 55: Barnaby's Picture Library, London. 56: Scala, Florence. 57: Foto Artothek, Bayerische Staatsgemäldesammlungen, Munich. 58: Foto Claus Hansmann, Munich. 59: Courtesy the Trustees of the British Library, London. 60: Belinda Wright/National Geographic Society. 61: Danny Turner, Dallas—Millicent Harvey, Boston. 62: Archives Tallandier, Paris. 63: Michael Holford Picture Library, London. 64: Jean-Loup Charmet, Paris. 65: From *Indian Dances of North America*, by Reginald and Gladys Laubin, University of Oklahoma Press, Norman, 1977. 66: Foto Claus Hansmann, Munich. 67: Rajesh Bedi, Rajouri Garden, New Delhi. 68, 69: D. Robin/Studio Paty, Nantes, France; Steve Rapport/LGI Photo Agency. 71-77: Art by Bryan Leister. 79: Francesco Pinton, Padua, Italy. 80: From *Picture Book of Devils, Demons and Witchcraft*, by Ernst and Johanna Lehner, Dover Publications, New York, 1971. 81: The Church of Satan, San Francisco. 82: The Art Institute of Chicago. 83: From *Picture Book of Devils, Demons and Witchcraft*, by Ernst and Johanna Lehner, Dover Publications, New York, 1971. 84: Founders Society, Detroit. 85: Culver Pictures, New York. 86: From *The Encyclopedia of Witchcraft and Demonology*, by Rossell Hope Robbins, Bonanza Books, New York, 1981. 87: Jean-Loup Charmet/Explorer, Paris. 88, 89: Joseph Anton Koch/Luisa Ricciarini, Milan; from *Devils*, by J. Charles Wall, EP Publishing Ltd., Yorkshire, England, 1974. 90: From *Devils*, by J. Charles Wall, EP Publishing Ltd., Yorkshire, England, 1974—Yves Coatsaliou/Sygma, New York. 91: J. L. Magneron, Sygma, New York. 92: Presseillustration Heinrich R. Hoffman, Munich. 93, 94: From *Devils*, by J. Charles Wall, EP Publishing Ltd., Yorkshire, England, 1974. 95: Jack and Betty Cheetham, San Antonio; from *Strange Cults*, by Angus Hall, Doubleday, Garden City, N.Y., 1976. 96: The Bettman Archive, New York. 97: Alexander Low/Woodfin Camp, New York. 98: Thomas L. Kelly, Wick, Littlehampton, West Sussex, England. 100, 101: Italo Bertolasi, Milan; Camerapix, London. 102, 103: David Alan Harvey © 1975 National Geographic Society; Graham Harrison, Startley, Wiltshire, England; Catherine Allemand/Gamma-Liaison, Paris. 104, 105: Thomas L. Kelly, Wick, Littlehampton, West Sussex, England; Ernst Fesseler, Ravensburg, Germany. 107: Ara Güler, Istanbul. 108: Charles Pereira, U.S. Park Police; AP/Wide World Photos. 110: Arturo Mari, Rome. 112, 113: Susan Griggs, London. 114: Mary Evans Picture Library, London. 117: Scala, Florence. 118: Wadsworth Atheneum, Hartford, the Ella Gallup Summer and Mary Catlin Summer Collection. 119: Dufoto, Rome. 121: Magnum, New York. 123: Art Zamur, Belgrade, Yugoslavia. 125: Freer Gallery, Smithsonian Institution, Washington, D.C. 126: Sygma Photo News, New York. 127: Mary Evans Picture Library, London. 129: Detail from center picture on pages 134, 135. 130: Otto Mü Verlag, Salzburg, Austria. 131: British Library, London. 132: Mary Evans Picture Library, London; Scala, Florence (2). 133: Gianni Dagli Orti, Paris. 134, 135: The National Gallery, London; Studio Basset, Caluire, Lyons, France; The National Gallery, London. 136, 137: The National Gallery, London; Staatliche Kunstsammlungen-Galerie Alte Meister, Dresden, Germany.

BIBLIOGRAPHY

Adler, Mortimer J., *The Angels and Us*. New York: Macmillan, 1982.

The Age of God-Kings: TimeFrame 3000-1500 BC (TimeFrame series). Alexandria, Va.: Time-Life Books, 1989.

Allen, Judy, and Jeanne Griffiths, *The Book of the Dragon*. London: Orbis, 1979.

Altizer, Thomas J. J., *Mircea Eliade and the Dialectic of the Sacred*. Philadelphia: Westminster Press, 1963.

Ariès, Philippe, *Images of Man and Death*. Transl. by Janet Lloyd. Cambridge, Mass.: Harvard University Press, 1985.

Baker, Roger, *Binding the Devil: Exorcism Past and Present*. London: Sheldon Press, 1974.

Bakhtiar, Laleh, *Sufi: Expressions of the Mystic Quest*. London: Thames and Hudson, 1976.

Becker, Ernest, *The Denial of Death*. New York: Macmillan, 1973.

Bedi, Rajesh, and John Keay, *Banaras: City of Shiva*. New Delhi, India: Brijbasi Printers, 1987.

Beer, Rüdiger Robert, *Unicorn: Myth and Reality*. Transl. by Charles M. Stern. New York: Van Nostrand Reinhold, 1972.

Berman, Morris, *Coming to Our Senses*. New York: Simon & Schuster, 1989.

Bernbaum, Edwin, "Wrathful Deities." *Parabola*, October 1981.

Berry, John W., "Temne and Eskimo Perceptual Skills." *International Journal of Psychology*, 1(3), 1966.

Bettelheim, Bruno, *The Uses of Enchantment*. New York: Random House, 1977.

Bloomfield, Morton W., *The Seven Deadly Sins*. East Lansing, Mich.: Michigan State College Press, 1952.

Bool, F. H., et al., *M. C. Escher: His Life and Complete Graphic Work*. Ed. by J. L. Locher, transl. by Tony Langham and Plym Peters. New York: Harry N. Abrams, 1981.

Boorstin, Daniel J., *The Discoverers*. New York: Random House, 1985.

Boros, Ladislaus, *Angels and Men*. Transl. by John Maxwell. New York: Seabury Press, 1976.

Bourget, Jean-Loup, "Painter of the Soul." *FMR* (English edition), September-October 1987.

Breeden, Stanley, "The First Australians." *National Geographic*, February 1988.

Brown, Edmund G., Jr., "Passage to India." *Life*, April 1988.

Burnham, Sophy, *A Book of Angels*. New York: Ballantine Books, 1990.

Caie, Norman MacLeod, *The Seven Deadly Sins*. New York: George H. Doran, 1923.

Campbell, Joseph:
The Hero with a Thousand Faces. Princeton, N.J.: Princeton University Press, 1947.
The Mythic Image. Princeton, N.J.: Princeton University Press, 1981.

Campbell, Joseph, with Bill Moyers, *The Power of Myth*. Ed. by Betty Sue Flowers. New York: Doubleday, 1988.

Cann, Rebecca L., "In Search of Eve." *The Sciences,* September-October 1987.

Carter, Robert, "The Tao and Mother Goose." *Parabola,* October 1981.

Casti, John L., *Paradigms Lost.* New York: William Morrow, 1989.

Cavendish, Richard, *Visions of Heaven and Hell.* London: Orbis, 1977.

Cavendish, Richard, ed., *Man, Myth & Magic.* New York: Marshall Cavendish, 1985.

Chesser, Eustace, *Sexual Behavior: Normal and Abnormal.* New York: Roy, 1949.

Clifton, Charles S., "The Three Faces of Satan: A Close Look at the Satanism Scare." *Gnosis,* summer 1989.

Colegrave, Sukie, *The Spirit of the Valley.* Los Angeles: J. P. Tarcher, 1979.

The Complete Grimm's Fairy Tales. Transl. by Margaret Hunt. New York: Random House, 1972.

Cooper, J. C., *Fairy Tales: Allegories of the Inner Life.* Wellingborough, Northamptonshire, England: Aquarian Press, 1983.

Cotterell, Arthur, *The Macmillan Illustrated Encyclopedia of Myths & Legends.* New York: Macmillan, 1989.

Crabtree, Adam, *Multiple Man.* New York: Praeger, 1985.

Crapanzano, Victor, and Vivian Garrison, eds., *Case Studies in Spirit Possession.* New York: Praeger, 1985.

Davidson, Gustav, *A Dictionary of Angels.* New York: Free Press, 1967.

Deutch, Richard, *Exorcism: Possession or Obsession.* London: Bachman & Turner, 1975.

Dundes, Alan, ed.:
Cinderella: A Casebook. New York: Wildman Press, 1983.
Little Red Riding Hood: A Casebook. Madison: University of Wisconsin Press, 1989.

Durden-Smith, Jo, and Diane deSimone, *Sex and the Brain.* New York: Arbor House, 1983.

Ebon, Martin, *The Devil's Bride: Exorcism Past and Present.* New York: Harper & Row, 1974.

Eisler, Riane, *The Chalice and the Blade.* San Francisco: Harper & Row, 1988.

Eliade, Mircea:
Shamanism: Archaic Techniques of Ecstasy. Transl. by Willard R. Trask. Princeton, N.J.: Princeton University Press, 1964.
The Two and the One. Transl. by J. M. Cohen. London: Harvill Press, 1965.

Eliade, Mircea, ed., *The Encyclopedia of Religion.* Vol. 5. New York: Macmillan, 1986.

Elson, Robert T., and the Editors of Time-Life Books, *Prelude to War* (World War II series). Alexandria, Va.: Time-Life Books, 1977.

Ernst, Bruno, *The Magic Mirror of M. C. Escher.* Transl. by John E. Brigham. New York: Random House, 1976.

Escher, M. C., *Escher on Escher: Exploring the Infinite.* Transl. by Karin Ford. New York: Harry N. Abrams, 1986.

Eysenck, Hans J., and Michael Eysenck, *Mindwatching: Why People Behave the Way They Do.* Garden City, N.Y.: Anchor Press, 1983.

Fairlie, Henry, *The Seven Deadly Sins Today.* Washington, D.C.: New Republic Books, 1978.

Fausto-Sterling, Anne, *Myths of Gender.* New York: Basic Books, 1985.

Feroli, Edward, "Putting Medjugorje 'Miracles' to the Test." *National Catholic Reporter,* December 30, 1988.

von Franz, Marie-Louise, *Problems of the Feminine in Fairytales.* Zürich: Spring Publications, 1972.

Freud, Sigmund, *Introductory Lectures on Psychoanalysis.* Transl. and ed. by James Strachey. New York: W. W. Norton, 1966.

Fuller, Graham, and Ian Knight, "The Lady Is a Pope?" *The Unexplained* (London), Vol. 13, Issue 151.

Gabriel, Trip, "Call of the Wildmen." *The New York Times Magazine,* October 14, 1990.

Gadon, Elinor W., *The Once and Future Goddess.* San Francisco: Harper & Row, 1989.

Gettings, Fred, *Secret Symbolism in Occult Art.* New York: Harmony Books, 1987.

Gilmore, G. Don, *Angels, Angels, Everywhere.* New York: Pilgrim Press, 1981.

Gimbutas, Marija, *The Language of the Goddess.* San Francisco: Harper & Row, 1989.

Goldberg, Philip, *The Intuitive Edge: Understanding and Developing Intuition.* Los Angeles: Jeremy P. Tarcher, 1983.

Goodman, Felicitas D., *The Exorcism of Anneliese Michel.* Garden City, N.Y.: Doubleday, 1981.

Grabois, Aryeh, *The Illustrated Encyclopedia of Medieval Civilization.* London: Octopus Books, 1980.

Graef, Hilda, *The Story of Mysticism.* Garden City, N.Y.: Doubleday, 1965.

Green, Richard, M.D., *Sexual Identity Conflict in Children and Adults.* New York: Basic Books, 1974.

Gregory, Richard L., ed., with O. L. Zangwill, *The Oxford Companion to the Mind.* New York: Oxford University Press, 1988.

Hahn, Emily, and Barton Lidice Beneš, *Breath of God.* Garden City, N.Y.: Doubleday, 1971.

Harner, Michael, *The Way of the Shaman.* Toronto: Bantam Books, 1982.

Hibbard, Howard, *Bernini.* Harmondsworth, Middlesex, England: Penguin Books, 1965.

Hildegard of Bingen and Matthew Fox, *Illuminations of Hildegard of Bingen.* Santa Fe, N.M.: Bear, 1985.

Hinnells, John R., *Persian Mythology.* Middlesex, England: Newnes Books, 1973.

Hobart, Billie, *Expansion.* New York: Glencoe, 1973.

Hook, Sidney, *Pragmatism and the Tragic Sense of Life.* New York: Basic Books, 1974.

Hunt, Morton, *The Compassionate Beast.* New York: William Morrow, 1990.

In the Image of Man (exhibition catalog). New York: Alpine Fine Arts Collection, March-June 1982.

Ions, Veronica, *Indian Mythology.* New York: Peter Bedrick Books, 1987.

James, William, *The Varieties of Religious Experience.* New York: Modern Library, 1936.

Janz, Denis R., "Medjugorje's Miracles: Faith and Profit." *Christian Century,* August 26-September 2, 1987.

Johnson, Kenneth Rayner:
The Fulcanelli Phenomenon. Jersey, Channel Islands, England: Spearman, 1980.
"The Image of Perfection." *The Unexplained* (London), Vol. 4, Issue 46.
"Transformation of an Alchemist." *The Unexplained* (London), Vol. 4, Issue 44.

Johnston, Jerry, *The Edge of Evil: The Rise of Satanism in North America.* Dallas: Word, 1989.

Jung, C. G., *Memories, Dreams, Reflections.* Ed. by Aniela Jaffé, transl. by Richard Winston and Clara Winston. New York: Random House, 1963.

Kelly, Edward, "We're Not Going to Make It." *Time,* January 25, 1982.

Kelly, Henry Ansgar, *The Devil, Demonology, and Witchcraft: The Development of Christian Beliefs in Evil Spirits.* Garden City, N.Y.: Doubleday, 1974.

Keuls, Eva C., *The Reign of the Phallus: Sexual Politics in Ancient Athens.* New York: Harper & Row, 1985.

Khanna, Madhu, *Yantra.* London: Thames and Hudson, 1979.

Kurtines, William M., and Jacob L. Gewirtz, *Morality, Moral Behavior, and Moral Development.* New York: John Wiley & Sons, 1984.

Kurtz, Paul:
Eupraxophy. Buffalo: Prometheus Books, 1989.
Forbidden Fruit. Buffalo: Prometheus Books, 1988.

Laubin, Reginald, and Gladys Laubin, *Indian Dances of North America: Their Importance to Indian Life.* Norman: University of Oklahoma Press, 1977.

Lebesque, Morvan, (pseud. Jean Hellé), *Miracles.* Transl. by Lancelot C. Sheppard. New York: David McKay, 1952.

Leigh, Richard, and Michael Baigent:
"The Goddess behind the Mask." *The Unexplained* (London), Vol. 1, Issue 6.
"Guardians of the Living Earth." *The Unexplained* (London), Vol. 1, Issue 8.
"Virgins with a Pagan Past." *The Unexplained* (London), Vol. 1, Issue 4.

Leroy, Olivier, *Levitation.* London: Oates & Washbourne, 1928.

Lewis, C. S., *Miracles.* London: Geoffrey Bles, 1947.

Locher, J. L., ed., *The World of M. C. Escher.* New York: Harry N. Abrams, 1971.

Lyons, Arthur, *Satan Wants You: The Cult of Devil Worship in America.* New York: Mysterious Press, 1988.

McClure, Kevin:
"Out of the Mouths of Babes." *The Unexplained* (London), Vol. 7, Issue 80.
"Visions of the Virgin." *The Unexplained* (London), Vol. 7, Issue 78.

McCombs, Phil, and Marianne Kyriakos. "Angels among Us." *Washington Post,* April 15, 1990.

McDannell, Colleen, and Bernhard Lang, *Heaven: A History.* New Haven, Conn.: Yale University Press, 1988.

McGee, Patricia, "Challenging History: Peaceful Women May Have Once Ruled the World." *Maclean's,* February 12, 1990.

McGrath, Peter, "Death on the Potomac." *Newsweek,* January 25, 1982.

Maclagan, David, *Creation Myths.* London: Thames and Hudson, 1977.

McMurran, Kristin, "A Canadian Woman's Bizarre Childhood Memories of Satan Shock Shrinks and Priests." *People,* September 1, 1980.

Martin, Malachi, *Hostage to the Devil: The Possession and Exorcism of Five Living Americans.* Pleasantville, N.Y.: Reader's Digest Press, 1976.

Mead, Margaret, *Sex and Temperament in Three Primitive Societies.* London: Routledge & Kegan Paul, 1952 (reprint of 1935 edition).

Miller, Hamish, and Paul Broadhurst, *The Sun and the Serpent.* Cornwall, England: Pendragon Press, 1989.

"The Miracle of Lourdes." *Geo,* June 1981.

Moir, Alfred, *Caravaggio.* New York: Harry N. Abrams, 1989.

Monden, Louis, *Signs and Wonders.* New York: Desclee, 1960.

Money, John, and Patricia Tucker, *Sexual Signatures.* Boston: Little, Brown, 1975.

Mookerjee, Ajit, *Ritual Art of India.* London: Thames and Hudson, 1985.

Moolenburgh, H. C., *A Handbook of Angels.* Saffron Walden, Essex, England: C. W. Daniel, 1984.

Morgan, Robin, comp. and ed., *Sisterhood Is Global*. Garden City, N.Y.: Doubleday, 1984.

"Movie of the Week: *The Picture of Dorian Gray*." *Life*, March 19, 1945.

Mullin, Redmond, *Miracles and Magic*. London: A. R. Mowbray, 1978.

Nazario, Sonia L., "Is Goddess Worship Finally Going to Put Men in Their Place?" *Wall Street Journal*, June 7, 1990.

Needham, Rodney, *Counterpoints*. Berkeley, Calif.: University of California Press, 1987.

"The Numbing of America." *Time*, January 25, 1982.

Oesterreich, Traugott K., *Possession and Exorcism*. New York: Causeway Books, 1974.

Opie, Iona, and Peter Opie, *The Classic Fairy Tales*. London: Oxford University Press, 1974.

Pagels, Elaine, *Adam, Eve, and the Serpent*. New York: Random House, 1988.

Perry, Nicholas, and Loreto Echeverría, *Under the Heel of Mary*. London: Routledge, 1988.

Phillips, John A., *Eve: The History of an Idea*. San Francisco: Harper & Row, 1984.

Powell, Andrew, and Graham Harrison, *Living Buddhism*. London: British Museum Publications, 1989.

Prince, Lydia, *Appointment in Jerusalem*. Chappaqua, N.Y.: Chosen Books, 1975.

"Psychiatrists to 'Treat' Satanism." *Washington Post*, September 7, 1989.

Purce, Jill, *The Mystic Spiral: Journey of the Soul*. London: Thames and Hudson, 1974.

Purtill, Richard L., Michael H. Macdonald, and Peter J. Kreeft, *Philosophical Questions*. Englewood Cliffs, N.J.: Prentice-Hall, 1985.

Rawson, Philip, *Tantra: The Indian Cult of Ecstasy*. London: Thames and Hudson, 1973.

Rawson, Philip, and Laszlo Legeza, *Tao*. London: Thames and Hudson, 1987.

Raymond, Janice G., *The Transsexual Empire*. Boston: Beacon Press, 1979.

Rhine, Louisa E., *Hidden Channels of the Mind*. New York: William Morrow, 1961.

Robbins, Rossell Hope, *The Encyclopedia of Witchcraft and Demonology*. New York: Bonanza Books, 1981.

Rodewyk, Adolf, S. J., *Possessed by Satan: The Church's Teaching on the Devil, Possession, and Exorcism*. New York: Doubleday, 1975.

Rogo, D. Scott, *Miracles*. New York: Dial Press, 1982.

Ronner, John, *Do You Have a Guardian Angel?* Indialantic, Fla.: Mamre Press, 1985.

Rosenblatt, Roger, "The Man in the Water." *Time*, January 25, 1982.

Rosenthal, Abigail L., *A Good Look at Evil*. Philadelphia: Temple University Press, 1987.

Ross, Nancy Wilson, *Three Ways of Asian Wisdom*. New York: Simon and Schuster, 1966.

Russell, Jeffrey B.:
 A History of Witchcraft. London: Thames and Hudson, 1980.
 Mephistopheles: The Devil in the Modern World. Ithaca, N.Y.: Cornell University Press, 1986.
 The Prince of Darkness. Ithaca, N.Y.: Cornell University Press, 1988.

Safran, Claire, "Hero of the Frozen River." *Reader's Digest*, September 1982.

Sagan, Eli, *Freud, Women, and Morality*. New York: Basic Books, 1988.

Sanford, John A., *Healing and Wholeness*. New York: Paulist Press, 1977.

Scharfstein, Ben-Ami, *Mystical Experience*. Indianapolis: Bobbs-Merrill, 1973.

Scollay, Clive, and Penny Tweedie, "Arnhem Land Aboriginals Cling to Dreamtime." *National Geographic*, November 1980.

Sharkey, John, *Celtic Mysteries*. New York: Crossroad, 1981.

Singer, June, *Androgyny: Toward a New Theory of Sexuality*. Garden City, N.Y.: Doubleday, 1976.

Stern, Karl, *The Flight from Woman*. New York: Paragon House, 1985.

Stone, Merlin:
 Ancient Mirrors of Womanhood. Vol. 1. New York: New Sibylline Books, 1979.
 When God Was a Woman. New York: Harcourt Brace Jovanovich, 1976.

Stout, Jeffrey, *Ethics after Babel*. Boston: Beacon Press, 1988.

Stutley, Margaret, *The Illustrated Dictionary of Hindu Iconography*. London: Routledge & Kegan Paul, 1985.

Thompson, William Irwin, *Imaginary Landscape*. New York: St. Martin's Press, 1989.

Thurston, Herbert:
 The Physical Phenomena of Mysticism. Ed. by J. H. Crehan. London: Burns & Oates, 1952.
 Surprising Mystics. Ed. by J. H. Crehan. London: Burns & Oates, 1955.

Unger, Rusty, "Oh Goddess!" *New York*, June 4, 1990.

Victor, Jeffrey S., "The Spread of Satanic-Cult Rumors." *Skeptical Inquirer*, spring 1990.

Walker, Barbara G., *The Woman's Encyclopedia of Myths and Secrets*. San Francisco: Harper & Row, 1983.

Ward, Theodora, *Men and Angels*. New York: Viking, 1969.

Watkins, Leslie, *The Real Exorcists*. London: Methuen, 1983.

Watts, Alan W.:
 Nature, Man, and Woman. New York: Random House, 1970.
 The Two Hands of God. New York: George Braziller, 1963.

Weigle, Marta, *Spiders & Spinsters: Women and Mythology*. Albuquerque: University of New Mexico Press, 1982.

Weiss, Michael, and Joyce Leviton, "Flight 90 Ends in Tragedy, Heroism and Miraculous Survival." *People*, February 1, 1982.

Westwood, Jennifer, ed., *The Atlas of Mysterious Places*. New York: Weidenfeld & Nicolson, 1987.

Williams, Walter L., *The Spirit and the Flesh*. Boston: Beacon Press, 1986.

Wilson, Edward O., *Sociobiology: The New Synthesis*. Cambridge, Mass.: Harvard University Press, 1975.

Wilson, Peter Lamborn, *Angels*. New York: Pantheon Books, 1980.

Woodward, Kenneth L., "Making Saints." *Newsweek*, November 12, 1990.

Yang Jwing-Ming, *Chi Kung*. Jamaica Plain, Mass.: Yang's Martial Arts Association, 1987.

Zaehner, R. C., *Matter and Spirit*. Vol. 8. New York: Harper & Row, 1963.

Zimmer, Heinrich, *Myths and Symbols in Indian Art and Civilization*. Ed. by Joseph Campbell. New York: Pantheon Books, 1953.

Zolla, Elémire, *The Androgyne*. London: Thames and Hudson, 1981.

INDEX

TIME-LIFE BOOKS

EDITOR-IN-CHIEF: Thomas H. Flaherty

Director of Editorial Resources: Elise D. Ritter-Clough
Executive Art Director: Ellen Robling
Director of Photography and Research: John Conrad Weiser
Editorial Board: Dale M. Brown, Janet Cave, Roberta Conlan, Robert Doyle, Laura Foreman, Jim Hicks, Rita Thievon Mullin, Henry Woodhead
Assistant Director of Editorial Resources: Norma E. Shaw

PRESIDENT: John D. Hall

Vice President and Director of Marketing: Nancy K. Jones
Editorial Director: Russell B. Adams, Jr.
Director of Production Services: Robert N. Carr
Production Manager: Prudence G. Harris
Supervisor of Quality Control: James King

Editorial Operations
Production: Celia Beattie
Library: Louise D. Forstall
Computer Composition: Deborah G. Tait (Manager), Monika D. Thayer, Janet Barnes Syring, Lillian Daniels
Interactive Media Specialist: Patti H. Cass

Time-Life Books is a division of Time Life Incorporated

PRESIDENT AND CEO: John M. Fahey, Jr.

Library of Congress Cataloging in Publication Data
Cosmic Duality / by the editors of Time-Life Books.
p. cm.—(Mysteries of the unknown)
Includes bibliographical references and index.
ISBN 0-8094-6516-7 (trade)
ISBN 0-8094-6517-5 (library)
1. Polarity—Miscellanea. 2. Polarity (Philosophy)—Miscellanea. 3. Polarity—Religious aspects—Miscellanea. 4. Dualism—Miscellanea.
I.Time-Life Books. II. Series.
BF1999.C6975 1991
147′.4—dc20   90-28806
                                                    CIP

MYSTERIES OF THE UNKNOWN

SERIES EDITOR: Jim Hicks
Series Administrator: Jane A. Martin
Art Director: Tom Huestis
Picture Editor: Paula York-Soderlund

Editorial Staff for *Cosmic Duality*
Text Editors: Janet Cave (principal), Robert A. Doyle
Senior Writer: Esther R. Ferington
Associate Editors/Research: Patti H. Cass, Sharon Obermiller
Assistant Editor/Research: Denise Dersin
Assistant Art Director: Susan M. Gibas
Writer: Sarah D. Ince
Copy Coordinators: Donna Carey, Colette Stockum
Picture Coordinator: Michael Kentoff
Editorial Assistant: Donna Fountain

Special Contributors: Jennifer Pearce (lead research); Mark Fabiano, Ann Louise Gates, Patricia A. Paterno, Nancy J. Seeger, Jacqueline Shaffer (research); Margery A. duMond, Rick Fields, Harvey S. Loomis, Jennifer Moses, Maria Mudd, John Neary, Mariah Burton Nelson, Jake Page, Susan Perry, Daniel Stashower, John Tompkins, William Trott, Robert White (text); Sara Schneidman (consultant); John Drummond (design); Hazel Blumberg-McKee (index).

Correspondents: Elisabeth Kraemer-Singh (Bonn), Christine Hinze (London), Christina Lieberman (New York), Maria Vincenza Aloisi (Paris), Ann Natanson (Rome).
Valuable assistance was also provided by Pavle Svabic (Belgrade); Angelika Lemmer (Bonn); Peter Hawthorne (Cape Town); Judy Aspinall (London); John Dunn (Melbourne); Andrea Dabrowski (Mexico City); Meenakshi Ganguly, Deepak Puri (New Delhi); Elizabeth Brown (New York); Ann Wise (Rome); Traudl Lessing (Vienna).

Consultants:
Marcello Truzzi, general consultant for the series, is a professor of sociology at Eastern Michigan University. He is also director of the Center for Scientific Anomalies Research (CSAR) and editor of its journal, the *Zetetic Scholar.* Dr. Truzzi, who considers himself a "constructive skeptic" with regard to claims of the paranormal, works through the CSAR to produce dialogues between critics and proponents of unusual scientific claims.

John B. Carlson worked in extragalactic and radio astronomy before developing a new interdisciplinary specialty, the study of astronomy in ancient cultures. Carlson concentrates on the astronomy of pre-Columbian America and is the founder and director of the Center for Archaeoastronomy in College Park, Maryland.

For information on and a full description of any of the Time-Life Books series listed above, please call 1-800-621-7026 or write:
Reader Information
Time-Life Customer Service
P.O. Box C-32068
Richmond, Virginia 23261-2068

This volume is one of a series that examines the history and nature of seemingly paranormal phenomena. Other books in the series include: